Sowing Seeds: The Militar
How to Cou

Edited by Owen

PUBLISHED BY WAR RESISTERS'
INTERNATIONAL

June 2013

ISBN 978-0-903517-27-0

THANKS

Many people were involved in making this book. In addition to all the article contributors and translators, and the Countering the Militarisation of Youth conference interviewees, thanks to:

Mitzi Bales, for all the help with the editing

Michael Schulze von Glaßer, for conducting and transcribing the Darmstadt interviews; Benno Malte Fuchs and Ralf Willinger for helping to conduct them; Natalia Pita Álvarez for doing the Spanish interpreting; and Paul Rankin, Rebecca House, Achim Schmitz, and Richard Meakin for translating the Spanish and German transcripts into English.

Sahar Vardi, for initiating - and helping to revise, distribute, and analyse - the survey; Hannah Brock and Ranaan Forshner for analysing the rest; Matias Mulet Truyols for translating it into Spanish; and the survey respondents* Kai-Uwe Dosch (Bund für Soziale Verteidigung, Germany), Oskar Castro, Joe Moore, Subhash Kattel (Alternatives to Violence Project, Nepal), Sahar Vardi, Shahaf Weisbein (New Profile, Israel), Eleni V, Angelos Nikolopoulos (Association of Greek COs), Union pacifiste de France, Conscientious Objectors of Tarn (France), Hawi Rapudo (Usalama Reforms Forum) and Dola Nicholas Oluoch (Chemchemi Ya Ukweli, Kenya), Alena Karaliova (Citizen.Army.Law, Russia), Sergey Krivenko, Jean De Wandelaer and Cecilia Moretti, Will McCallum and David Gee (ForcesWatch, UK), Stefan Dietiker (Gruppe für eine Schweiz ohne Armee) and Piet Dörflinger (zivildienst.ch, Switzerland), Kolectivo Antimilitarista Medellín and Acción Colectiva de Objetores y Objetoras de Conciencia (Colombia), World Without War (South Korea), Ellen Elster (Folkereisning Mot Krig, Norway), Vidal Acevedo (Servicio Paz y Justicia, Paraguay), Xavier Leon Vega (Grupo de Objeción de Conciencia Ecuador), Julene Eiguren Gandarias (Alternativa Antimilitarista MOC, Basque Country), Carlos Barranco, Roel Stynen (Vredesactie) and Ludo De Brabander (Vrede, Belgium), Sheehan Moore, Amine Ay, Hechem El Jed, Remígio and Ivo Chilaule, Paavo Kolttola, Juho Narsakka (Aseistakieltäytyjäliitto, Finland), Ofog (Sweden), Javiera Rosa, Serge Vandenberghe, Laura Pollecutt and Rob Thomson (Ceasefire Campaign, South Africa), Boro Kitanoski (Peace Action), Igor Seke and Petar Milicevic, and others. (*only where a group/organisation is named on its own are the responses that of the group/organisation)

Hilal Demir, for the cover design

Jessica Metheringham, Michèle Brock, Graham Everett, and Jenny McCarthy for proofreading the final draft

Javier Garate for the help with the layout

The Right to Refuse to Kill Committee for their general advice and support

and Bertha-von-Suttner Stiftung (DVG-VK), Fraktionsverein die Linke, Geneva Quaker Meeting Social Appeals Committee, GEW HV (Germany), Rosa Luxemburg Stiftung, and Sebastian Cobler Stiftung, for contributing to the funding of the 2012 Countering the Militarisation of Youth conference, which included an amount for the publication of this book.

CONTENTS

4

Introduction

Sergeiy Sandler

What are the causes of war? Typical answers to this question feature stories about politicians, national claims, religions, or bit ideologies with an 'ism' in their name. More sophisticated answers would mention economic interests and the exploitation of natural resources. But even the best explanations of this sort do not yet show the full picture; they do not amount to a sufficient cause for war. For a war to be waged, sufficiently many people have to actively wage it and sufficiently many people have to passively accept and condone it. And since war is not a particularly pleasant business, an effort has to be made to educate people to accept war, to prepare for it, and to fight in it, preferably from a young age.

The seeds of militarisation are planted and replanted long in advance to yield the crop of conflict and war and provide a supply of human and material resources to the world's armies. Emma Sangster, in her article in this book, quotes a frank statement by the former head of recruitment strategy in the British Army, Col. David Allfrey, to this effect:

> Our new model is about raising awareness and that takes a ten-year span. It starts with a seven-year-old seeing a parachutist at an air show and thinking, "That looks great." From then the army is trying to build interest by drip, drip, drip.[1]

Sowing Seeds: The Militarisation of Youth and How to Counter It is a book about these seeds of war, planted in the minds of children, adolescents, and young adults. It is also a book about another kind of seeds—the seeds of resistance to this military drip—which, we hope, it will help disseminate around the world.[2] The book comes out of an international conference—the first of its kind[3], and, we hope, the first in a series—of activists working to counter the militarisation of youth, held in Darmstadt, Germany, in June 2012.

The participants of the conference, and the authors of the articles collected in this book, come from organisations that work against war, and especially against the militarist culture of war, in different countries. Naturally, many of the participants came from the host country, Germany, where there is a recent surge of activism against military presence in schools and universities (to counter the surge in such military presence, following the current transition of the German military from conscription to voluntary recruitment). But a lot of the conference participants came from other countries in Europe, the Americas, the Middle East and Africa. Many of the conference's presentations and workshops are documented in this book.

What was immediately striking about the exchange of experiences that happened in Darmstadt was the extent to which our experiences resembled one another. It became apparent that across political and cultural contexts and despite differences in recruitment models (universal conscription, lottery draft, volunteer recruitment), a surprisingly uniform array of tools is being used to militarise young minds. Similarly, although each of the articles in this volume focuses on the situation in a different country and on different forms and aspects of militarism, we find several recurrent themes running through all of them.

War and conflict—historical, recent, and current—is always part of the context, as is the strong link between militarism and nationalism: national symbols, holidays, ceremonies, are often given distinctly military attributes (especially in the more highly militarised countries, which maintain active armed conflicts on or within their borders), focusing on heroism and on the wars of the past, present, and future. Ceremonies, memorials, and other forms of commemoration (for example the naming of schools and streets), whether done by the military itself or by civilian authorities, often have clear military characteristics and are linked to battles, military leaders, and soldiers killed in action. These play an important role in how children and young people are socialised.

In addition, of course, the education system plays a central role in the militarisation of youth, and of society as a whole. As Serdar M. Değirmencioğlu explains in his article:

> Schools around the world provide fertile ground for militarism: there is a captive audience, a comprehensive mandate, a hierarchical structure and a clear power differential between students and professionals. Schools can easily be turned into paramilitary institutions.

And indeed, in country after country, we see reports of school children (sometimes even primary and pre-school age) being dressed in military uniforms for one ceremony or another, being given military training - sometimes including training in the handling of weapons - being encouraged to play with or around weapons systems such as tanks, and being subjected to rules of school discipline that closely emulate military ones.

And while in some countries, such as Germany, we find similar measures being introduced (or rather, reintroduced) to promote recruitment to armed forces as they phase out conscription, in others, such as Turkey, Chile, and Israel, militarised education and society works hand in hand with a system of conscription or mandatory recruitment by draft, to create societies that willingly accept war, conflict, and military dominance in government.

This strong sense, which we all experienced when we met at the Darmstadt conference, that in different countries and contexts we are all facing a common problem led to a joint effort to document militarisation of youth practices around the world and available avenues for resisting them. In this book, at the beginning of each chapter, you will find analyses of the relevant parts of a worldwide survey of thirty-two countries (begun at the Darmstadt conference and revised and expanded over the following months) on the militarisation practices affecting young people around the world[4] and relevant extracts from transcripts of interviews (all conducted at Darmstadt) with sixteen activists from around the world on the situation in their countries. The survey coaxes out some of the international and intranational variations in the militarisation of youth – for example, how armed forces' use of social media for recruitment and publicity is less in countries without prevalent internet access, and how Quebec differs from the rest of Canada, respectively. The full results of the survey can be found on the War Resisters' International website, at: http://wri-irg.org/surveydata. Links to additional resources on the subject are gathered on the Resources page at the end of this book.

Overview of the articles in this book

The militarisation of youth is evident in school settings and occurs explicitly at recruitment fairs, but it also involves a military presence in the physical environment people live in. This militarisation of space is the subject of the articles in the first chapter, 'Overt and Covert Recruitment: The Militarisation of Public and Private Space'.

David Gee, in '"Catch them young before the army loses them"', looks at recruitment, especially in countries without conscription. Focusing particularly on the situation in the UK, Gee pays special attention to how the military targets young people from the most disadvantaged groups in society for recruitment, and notes the higher price members of these groups pay for the 'favour', compared to other members of the armed forces.

'The militarisation of everyday lives in Venezuela' is the topic of Rafael Uzcategui's article. Uzcategui focuses particularly on the ways in which military practices have become part of civilian life in his country: the military attributes of civilian ceremonies, military presence in schools, but also increased military control over universities and the formation of military-like structures in colleges and workplaces.

In 'Publicity campaigns: The German Armed Forces' struggle for the hearts and minds of the population' – the first of his two contributions – Michael Schulze von Glaßer looks at recruitment efforts through the military's presence in public spaces and the media (ceremonies, adverts), focusing on the changes in this presence brought about by the transition of the German armed forces from conscription to voluntary recruitment.

The military's presence in public space is also the subject of the next article,

'Invisible militarism in Israel', by Ruti Kantor and Diana Dolev. Kantor and Dolev note the ubiquitous military presence in this very highly militarised society, by no means limited to events and adverts initiated by the military itself, which often becomes all but invisible to the population exposed to it.

Boro Kitanoski's 'Monuments and memory in Former Yugoslavia' focuses on a highly potent and broadly used instrument of militarisation: the physical features and social contextualisation of war monuments. The example of Former Yugoslav countries in the Balkans is especially instructive in showing how monuments of past wars can be used to perpetuate conflicts in the present and into the future.

'On-screen warfare', Michael Schulze von Glaßer's second article, focuses on one rarely-addressed but very significant aspect of the militarisation of youth: the glorification of war in video games. The video game industry has many formal and informal ties to the world's amed forces and it appeals to a huge number of young people (especially adolescent males—a favourite target of military recruiters) with simplistic pro-war messages. Schulze von Glaßer also discusses some attempts to create video games with alternative messages as one possible avenue for countering the gaming industry's militarisation of youth.

Finally, Jorge Veléz, in 'The impact of war and the para-state in Colombia', examines the militarisation of young people's environments from another angle. The price of increased violence in highly militarised and war-torn societies—as Veléz reminds us—is borne disproportionately by the youth, both as perpetrators and as victims.

The second part of the book, 'Shaping the Debate: Militarising Public Discourse and Education', shifts from examining the militarisation of young people's physical and social environment to the militarisation of minds and values. The arguments and values used by the armed forces and the state to convince the public of the necessity of war and to fool young people into joining the military are examined by Jonna Schürkes in '"Die for your country": Turning to bravery, loyalty and honour in order to legitimise war and recruit soldiers in Germany.' Although she focuses on the current situation in Germany, many details will no doubt sound familiar to readers from any country.

A detailed examination of the history and current practices of militarisation – especially within the school system – in Turkey, can be found in Serdar Değirmenciolu's article, 'Young people in Turkey besieged by militarism: Past and present.' Değirmenciolu offers a very telling panorama of how the militarisation of youth works in a highly militarised society. Again, despite the specific historical context being that of Turkey, the practices described are part of the experience of children around the world.

While several of the articles by German authors in this book note the resurgence of military presence in German public space and education system following the shift from mandatory to voluntary recruitment in the country, Dan Contreras, in 'Violence, military service, and the education system in Chile', draws attention to the fact that a mandatory recruitment system, as in Chile, can also actively use propaganda to attract recruits and to legitimise the ongoing armed conflict that the state maintains (in this case, with an indigenous group in the south of Chile).

Finally, Emma Sangster, in 'The military's influence in UK education', documents the recent surge in military presence in young people's lives in the UK, and especially in schools, as part of a concentrated effort by recent British governments (regardless of the identity of the ruling party). Sangster stresses that the armed forces are generally presented as an uncontroversial actor in education, and how military discipline is marketed as a positive alternative to the perceived failure of regular schools, especially in poorer areas.

There is a close and deep connection between gender and militarism. An analysis of militarisation and recruitment from a feminist and queer perspective is the focus of the third part of the book. In their articles, Andreas Speck ('Queer and gender critiques of military recruitment and militarisation') and Sahar M. Vardi ('"One of the boys": The conscription of young women to the Israeli military') both examine the military and military recruitment from a gender perspective. They point out the inherently patriarchal and heterosexist nature of military systems and the prevalence of sexual harassment, assault, and hazing in all militaries. They also consider the purposes served by Western armed forces' efforts to exhibit a façade of openness and recruit women and queers. 'This illusion of equality has two purposes', explains Vardi. One is simply to expand the military's ranks. The other has to do with framing these armies' 'enemies' as intolerant and hostile to liberal values, or as Speck puts it: 'It forms part of the anti-Muslim propaganda, rather than being a reflection of a genuinely open military that is friendly to women and queers.' Nor can a military be friendly to women and queers. The two articles remind us that the feminist and queer struggles are about changing society, not about finding a place for women and queers within the current patriarchal order and the military (its purest manifestation).

The seeds of war are sown in abundance, but so are the seeds of resistance. The last section of this book looks at ways to counter the militarisation of youth. Kelly Dougherty, in 'The role of military veterans and current service members', tells about the work of Iraq Veterans against the War, the organisation she co-founded and continues to be involved with in the United States. A central part of this work involves war veterans visiting schools and colleges to share their experiences from their own military service, countering the myths, lies, and half-truths being sold to school and college students by military recruiters. As Dougherty explains:

> The simple act of telling the story of your military experience, your

experience in a war zone, and the difficulties you face when you come home and leave the military, can have a profound effect on young people who have never heard anyone talk about their military service outside of the patriotic, black and white lens of the military establishment.

She also devotes attention to the challenges of involving war veterans—most of whom are not, to begin with, familiar with activist culture, and many of whom suffer from trauma that needs to be recognised and allowed to heal—in antimilitarist activism.

In the next article, 'Resisting the militarisation of education', Kai-Uwe Dosch, Sarah Roßa and Lena Sachs focus on examples of (at least partly) successful intervention by students, teachers, and activists against the military presence in German schools – approaches which could be used in other countries too. The armed forces, at least in Germany, fear controversy: 'The armed forces are not at all immune to protests; they can be made to retreat'.

Ralph Willinger, in 'Child rights: Using international law and the UN', explains about the main international legal instruments and procedures (especially under the Convention on the Rights of the Child) that can be used to counteract the militarisation of youth. Willinger illustrates the potential benefits of using these legal mechanisms as tools for building up political pressure and facilitating campaigns with the example of the shadow reports submitted by German organisations to the UN Committee on the Rights of the Child whenever Germany comes under review at this committee.

Cecil Arndt's article, 'Direct action against militarism', explores the use of nonviolent direct action to counter war and militarism more generally, emphasising the need to challenge militarism as a whole, not just the militarisation of young people, although some of the ideas and tactics Arndt mentions can also be used to confront youth-focused practices of militarisation such as the military presence in schools.

Finally, Cattis Laska and Hanns Molander, in 'The need for a queer perspective', present the work their group Ofog (Sweden) does to counter the militarisation of youth. Their actions include both educational activities, such as workshops for school students, and more direct (and creative) actions that disrupt military recruitment efforts, including ad-busting and street theatre at recruitment stalls. All these actions—Laska and Molander explain—reflect a gender analysis from a queer perspective, of militarism in general, and of the militarisation of youth in particular.

Sharing information about how the militarisation of youth operates and sharing tactics for countering it is an important early step in the struggle for peace, not just as a transient break between wars, but as a condition naturally attained by a society that does not militarise its young minds - a society which could be aptly described by this famous line from the bible: 'neither shall they learn war any more'. That goal is probably still very far away. For now we are just sowing seeds.

Notes

1   Cited in Stephen Armstrong, 'Britain's Child Army', *New Statesman*, 5 February 2007. <www.newstatesman.com/politics/2007/02/british-army-recruitment-iraq> (accessed 24 May 2013).
2   The title of the book was inspired by Hilal Demir's cover design.
3   As a precursor, one may note the more academic Militarism in Education: A Critical View conference held in Israel in May 2001.
4   For each country we almost always had at least two different respondents. All of the respondents are well-informed about the situation in their country, and researched their answers carefully, but some of the questions are subjective: we do not claim that the survey is a scientific study.

Overt and Covert Recruitment: The Militarisation of Public and Private Space

Survey findings: Recruitment

In the majority of the thirty-two countries surveyed[1], minors (those under 18 years old) cannot join the armed forces. However, there are multiple exceptions to this – such as the USA, France and Canada, whose military includes 17 year olds. In those countries that allow minors, there are often restrictions. In the UK, under-18s cannot serve in combat roles, and in Germany 17.5 year olds can join only with parental consent. In those states that do not officially allow minors to serve, this does sometimes happen nonetheless, for example in Israel and Colombia.

Many European states surveyed - Spain, Serbia, Macedonia, Germany and Sweden - fit the trend of numerous European states having abolished compulsory military service in the last 15 years. Austrians voted to keep it in a January 2013 referendum; a Swiss referendum will take place later this year. The vast majority of those surveyed countries with conscription recruit males only. All countries – with the exception of South Korea, Turkey, and northern Cyrpus – claim to offer the right to conscientious objection. However, it is often difficult to obtain. Outside of Europe, South Korea is the only country surveyed that does not provide for conscientious objection to military service. Compulsory substitute service exists in Paraguay, Switzerland, Russia, Greece, Finland, Austria and the Republic of Cyprus. In Cyprus, Finland and Switzerland, this substitute service is longer than the military service, contrary to international standards, which ensure that substitute service is not 'punitive' (including in terms of length). In Paraguay, if you wish to avoid this substitute service, you pay a daily fine.

A significant majority of countries ask their young people to register themselves for conscription. An anomaly is France: although there is no conscription, young people have to complete - usually between the ages of 16-18 - a 'Defence and Citizenship day' (otherwise they can't get a driving licence, or a degree).

Over two-thirds have local or national authorities that hand over young peoples' information to the military. This varies in terms of how systematic it is. In nine countries, information is also passed from schools to the military.

Twenty-two of the countries are involved in active combat, mostly externally - sometimes as part of a wider multilateral force such as NATO – but internally in Colombia, Ecuador, Paraguay, and India, which is an example of non-state militarisation of youth.

There are a number of aspects of the military that are emphasised to the public, partly to facilitate recruitment by presenting the armed forces in a positive light:

- Adventure: The military presents itself as providing adventure in its recruitment and other advertising in countries across all continents surveyed – although by no means all. In some, this appears to be a long-term tactic. In others, this is a recent or temporary policy. This is sometimes related to country-specific contexts, for example the Canadian armed forces emphasise how travel away from Canada otherwise is prohibitively expensive.

- Humanitarian and aid work: In all but eight countries, the military also does humanitarian and aid work. In Paraguay, this is heavily emphasised; in Nepal it isn't, yet this remains the public's perception of what they do.

- The military brings peace: Twenty of the militaries promote the belief that the military brings peace. This manifests itself in different ways: in Finland, the strength of their army is believed to prevent Russian aggression, while in Canada, there exists a popular view that the army are essentially peacekeepers, not a 'real military'.

- The military defends you and your values: Overwhelmingly in Europe, and noticeable in all other continents, is the view that the military defends the country and its values. Again Canada is an exception, with the emphasis being on helping others (partly because there has not been military organised armed conflict in the state of Canada).

- The military can be a career: In all but two countries surveyed - Turkish-administered Northern Cyprus and Nepal - this is one of the messages utilised.

- The military will lead to future study or employment opportunities: Similarly, the potential garnered by a military career is highlighted in many countries. This link is more or less explicit: in Canada, the military pay university costs ($7000 tuition, $10,000 living expenses each year), and in Turkey you cannot get government jobs without having served in the military. In South Africa, this is perceived as the main attraction.

- Other: In the US, the focus is on good health and the good pay; the latter argument is also prominent in Macedonia. In Spain it is a way for immigrants to attain citizenship, and in India the role of the military in responding to riots and other internal problems is emphasised.

Notes

1   Austria, Argentina, Belgium, Canada, Colombia, Cyprus (Republic of), Cyprus (Turkish-administered Northern), Ecuador, Finland, France, Germany, Greece, India, Ireland (Republic of), Israel, Kenya, Macedonia, Mozambique, Nepal, Norway, Paraguay, Russia, Serbia, South Africa, South Korea, Spain, Sweden, Switzerland, Tunisia, Turkey, UK, USA.

Quotes from WRI's Countering the Militarisation of Youth conference

> The way that I ended up joining the military was that when I was a senior in high school I intended to go to college but I didn't have any way to pay for it...I talked to an army recruiter [about an army scholarship] and he made it sound really good...Any time between signing the contract and going to basic training, you can change your mind and there won't be any consequences. Of course, the recruiters won't tell you that – they'll threaten legal consequences etc... - Kelly Dougherty, USA

> Adults – mature people – were not recruited into the military. Why recruit children? They recruited children because children are vulnerable, docile and can easily be brain-washed. Children don't think before they act. All they hear is "go". They act like robots. - Domino Frank Suleiman, Liberia

> The military has really been nothing more than a career for people in Canada. It hasn't been an ideological force, because we don't have to protect our borders; we've never had wars that are our own. So the military recruits mostly in high school from students who...come from low economic backgrounds, and also from rural areas where traditional industries have collapsed... - Christel LeBlanc, Canada

> There's one big factor that makes youth develop so much interest in enlistment: poverty. That is the key term, because we have got a high rate of unemployment... - Samuel Koduh, Ghana

> Adventure and technology play the biggest roles in advertisements aimed at young people. Things like the trauma and injuries Dutch troops returning from Afghanistan are experiencing are

obviously not addressed. - Geart Bosma, Netherlands

2012 was the first year since the military reform in 2000 that the volunteer quota hasn't been fulfilled...So the the advertising campaign has focused more on looking for the "heroic soldier", by promoting the idea of the helpful soldier who, for example, helped a lot in the earthquake catastrophe in 2010. - Dan Contreras, Chile

They cover the whole range from cinema, TV, printed material like brochures, and much more now on Facebook, YouTube. They also go into schools, they hold village fêtes, they have military parades, big military ceremonies. They attach military ceremonies to various other national events like the Olympics... – David Gee, UK

Survey findings: The military in public and private space

There is a mixed picture in terms of how much the military is visible on the streets. The ubiquity of some militaries is related to military service, whilst in other countries without conscription the presence of the military is limited to specific locations, for example train stations and near borders. Militarised actors like armed police are often present, in some countries where the military is not publicly visible (for example in the UK).

A minority of the countries have paramilitary or 'illegal' weapons visible on the street – in France, Paraguay and South Africa this includes 'security' personnel. Almost two thirds of the countries have heavy artillery in public spaces. This was mostly decommissioned, and for use in parades, with the exception of rural Switzerland and government building in Tunisia.

Five countries - Ecuador, Colombia, Switzerland, Israel, Finland – have bomb shelters in every building or street. Every single country surveyed – with the exception of Nepal – has streets or squares named after military figures of personnel. Mostly, these don't relate to recent conflicts.

All but three countries have military parades in public spaces, mostly on national holidays. In all but three countries that have an air force, the air force does exhibition flights. In Greece, the number of these has reduced since the financial crisis. In almost half of countries, members of the public (not including the family of military personnel) are allowed to visit military bases.

In twenty-three countries, the military has a presence at festivals and concerts, but the frequency of this varies. Slightly fewer – twenty-one – militaries actually organise their own festivals and concerts for the public. Only in Norway does the military not take part in national or religious or cultural celebrations. Twenty-seven countries also have monuments dedicated to military personnel in public spaces.

Quotes from WRI's Countering the Militarisation of Youth conference

I come from Hebron where there are some hundreds of Israeli settlers in the heart of the city who are protected by about 4,000 soldiers from the Israeli army. If you go to the old town you see soldiers everywhere. If you go to another town you see soldiers at the checkpoints. The Israeli military is everywhere...Palestine does not have its own armed forces, only police...although according to estimates Hamas [the Palestinian political party] has around 17,000 soldiers in the Gaza Strip. - Fadi Zatari, Palestine

National holidays are exploited by the military as a chance to showcase themselves in city centres. Sometimes they exhibit tanks in market squares. There are also open days for all branches of military services, which are very popular. Children have the chance to shoot with real rifles there. This obviously gets them excited. - Geart Bosma, Netherlands

If you look at the international airport in Ghana, it's named after one military man: General Kotoka. During Independence Day celebrations the military are there, parading, and the president inspects them. - Samuel Koduh, Ghana

The army gets conscripts to collect money for veteran organisations, so quite often you can see them in the streets in their army uniform collecting money... - Paavo Kolttola, Finland

You see soldiers on the streets all the time, with their weapons, going home. In May 2012 I saw a picture from a beer festival of a girl in her bikini, with her M-16 [rifle]...we're very much used to seeing weapons, literally everywhere. - Sahar Vardi, Israel

With the monuments...it's continuing the war with different tools. It's continuing with victims. Continuing this war mentality after the fighting is over. And the special problem with monuments is that they will stay for a very long time. - Boro Kitanoski, Macedonia

Since the end of conscription in 2010 the military has a lot of advertising on public transport, in public spaces – at specific events like the Stockholm Pride Festival and other festivals and happenings where there's a lot of people in central town, and also on social media – YouTube, Spotify, Facebook, and other online forums - because they want to attract young people. - Cattis Laska, Sweden

Colombia has a strong military and police presence on the streets, with automatic weapons, because we are in a state of war...you end up accepting the armed presence as an everyday occurrence. - Jorge Veléz, Colombia

They're actually targetting people below the recruitment age in order to get them ready for a military career before they reach recruitment age. And one of the ways they're doing that is by developing computer games of various kinds, to encourage a view of warfare as something that's exciting and glamourous. - David Gee, UK

The people working on developing Battlefield 3 went with the Swedish soldiers in Afghanistan to get a real picture of the war, and to implement that into their video/computer games. - Cattis Laska, Sweden

'Catch them young before the army loses them'[1]

David Gee

Ask a teacher what her purpose is and how she goes about it, and you can expect a simple answer: she supports young people to grow by teaching them things. We know why we need bakers, too; they feed people by baking us bread. So what are soldiers[2] for?

Their purpose, say the politicians who choose which wars are fought, is to defend the nation. In fact, most soldiers do little defending. All recent wars involving European or North American forces have been conflicts of choice; in the former Yugoslavia, Iraq and Afghanistan, Western states have initiated invasive wars by projecting military power far from home. There is no public consensus on whether these actions reflected the wise and courageous intentions of dispassionately humanitarian people, or bids to shape the geopolitics of the world for the benefit of its most powerful states. History shows that there are several purposes of armed forces, of which some are possibly benign but not self-evidently so, and others are plain malevolent. In effect, the soldier's purpose in war is not always, or even usually, to defend the nation, but rather to help win whatever struggle his political leadership has decided to wage.

The purpose of armed forces may be vague; the soldier's role in it is not, even if this is rarely spelt out. It is no use looking for a description of the soldier's role in military recruitment literature. The brochure for the British Infantry, for example, describes the infantryman's job as to 'defeat the enemy', 'engage an enemy', 'engage the target', make 'decisive strikes'[3] – all fantasy euphemisms as nonsensical as a baker who 'facilitates nutrition' or a teacher who 'pedagogicalises information'. If the teacher teaches and the baker bakes, then the soldier soldiers. What does this involve? General Michael Rose, who commanded UN forces in Bosnia, is unusual among his peers in his frankness: 'No other group in society is required either to kill other human beings, or expressly sacrifice themselves for the nation.'[4] Essentially, the soldier's job is to kill or threaten to kill (a word absent from the 12,000-word Infantry brochure) and accept the risk of being killed or injured. This is just as true of humanitarian peacekeepers – their guns are not loaded for nothing.

Recruiting the most vulnerable

Given that the purpose of armed forces is not self-evidently benign and that the job of soldiers is a mortally dangerous one primarily requiring the killing of other people, who would freely choose to make this their career choice? Put another way: how do the social and political elite of nation states persuade enough people

21

to fight their wars?

The answer is that they take an interest, hitherto probably lacking, in those social groups whose life options are fewest and whose choices are made from a position of relative weakness. These are young people who remain impressionable and have yet to develop the psychological maturity of adulthood. They are poor people whose education has been sub-standard, who have few civilian job opportunities available, and who may have young families to support. And they are people from ethnic minority groups at a social disadvantage when compared with the mainstream majority.

If you are all three – young, poor and from a minority background – then the armed forces are very likely to come calling. They will come to your school, your neighbourhood, your local unemployment agency. They will find you through adverts on TV, at the cinema, and on Facebook. They will offer you glossy leaflets, internet games, military clubs to join, and a chance to sit in a battle tank, hold a rifle or feel the controls of a fighter bomber. They will start this while you are still too young to enlist. When you are old enough to join the forces, they will promise you adventure, a developing career, new friends, a feeling of personal power, and a sense – often for the first time for many potential recruits – of belonging with others to a cause. They are not there to exploit your weak social position, they will insist, but to offer you a chance to strengthen it. The state, largely responsible for the social conditions of poverty in which you live, will now save you from them by giving you a job. Their rhetoric is that of having done you a favour, albeit one that very few people a little older than you or from a more privileged background would accept.

The cover of the 2006 British Army recruiters' guide for parents has a doctored photograph of a graduation 'passing out' parade for parents, where ethnically diverse faces have been inserted to attract families of potential recruits from non-white backgrounds (credit – David Gee)

The realities of military life

The reality of armed forces life is nothing like the brochures and online ads. New recruits in all countries become subject to special national and international laws that nullify many civil, political and human rights, such as the right not to be required to perform forced or compulsory labour.[5] The legal obligations of enlistment prevent those who want to leave from doing so (for four years or more in the UK[6]); soldiers may be incarcerated if they try and many have been. Young people from the poorest neighbourhoods targeted by recruiters[7] typically have underdeveloped literacy skills, which puts them at a disadvantage when trying to understand the complex commitments involved in order to make a free and informed choice.

Some recruits are happy with their career choice and will stay that way, but although statistics from the UK show that there are more happy soldiers than unhappy ones, job satisfaction is still lower in the armed forces than in civilian life.[8] Whether or not they like their new job, armed forces recruits face a barrage of physical and psychological risks. British and US studies show that mental health problems in the military are higher than in the general population, with much higher levels of harmful alcohol use, appreciably higher rates of post-traumatic stress disorder (PTSD), and similar or slightly higher rates of anxiety and depression.[9] Deployment to war zones increases the risks further, especially for those in direct combat roles such as the Infantry and those who enlisted young and from disadvantaged backgrounds.[10] As exposure to warfare increases or intensifies, traumatic events such as being shot at, handling dead bodies, seeing someone being killed, and killing or wounding other people, again increase the prevalence of clinically significant mental health problems.[11] Young recruits from disadvantaged backgrounds are much more vulnerable to these risks.[12] In the UK, soldiers who enlisted at the youngest age (16) have been substantially more likely to lose their lives in Afghanistan that those who enlisted aged 18 or above[13]; given that the risk of being injured has been about five times that of being killed[14], recruits enlisting younger also face a higher risk of non-fatal injury. In the British and US context, and probably elsewhere as well, the youngest recruits from the most disadvantaged neighbourhoods are also most likely to occupy the most dangerous roles, such as in the Infantry, because these jobs are relatively unskilled and require fewer or no qualifications.[15] Even at times of low deployment, the youngest recruits are more likely to be bullied and, especially if female, sexually harassed.[16]

The overall picture is that the youngest people from the poorest backgrounds are both most vulnerable to mental health problems and also most likely to occupy military roles with high levels of exposure to traumatic events. For example, one British study found that 17.5% of personnel under twenty years of age had symptoms of PTSD in the Gulf War[17] and another found that the prevalence of PTSD symptoms among those who joined the armed forces with no qualifications (these are likely to have enlisted youngest, including straight from school) was 18.4%.[18] These rates of PTSD are far higher than the 3.0% found in the general UK population.[19] Equally striking is that harmful alcohol use in the youngest military age group, and in recruits from the most disadvantaged backgrounds, has been found to be three times as prevalent as in the general population.[20] The common assumption that recruiting disadvantaged youngsters is good for them just does not stand up to scrutiny.

The situation elsewhere

Since conditions in the British and US armed forces have much in common with those of other industrialised states, it is likely that young people in other countries also face heightened psychological and physical risks when compared with adult recruits or the general population.

When nine of us, each from a different country[21], explored this issue in a workshop at the Countering the Militarisation of Youth conference in Darmstadt, we all described similar armed forces recruitment tactics: active marketing to young people, especially from poor communities; the glamourisation of military jobs as a route to an adventurous life, especially by presenting the soldier, sailor or airman as a hyper-masculine role; and the omission or glossing over of the substantial risks and difficulties involved. All of us were concerned about this militarisation of youth and the harm it causes to young people's wellbeing for the sake of armed violence orchestrated by the elite class of the older generation.

In all our countries apart from Switzerland, military recruitment has flourished in conditions of local poverty and/or episodes of national economic crisis, where there are few civilian job options available. In most countries, a job in the armed forces is the only apparent way for some male bread-winners to be able to provide for their families; this is especially the case in poorer countries like Ghana or very unequal societies like South Africa. Recruitment is also successful where there is a high level of national pride in the state armed forces, which spend large sums to encourage this sentiment through parades, advertising and national days to celebrate themselves.

In all the countries of which we had experience (except, again, Switzerland), the armed forces actively target their marketing at the youngest recruits. Whilst the emphasis in general remains on appealing to boys of school-leaving age, most armed forces now also have dedicated programmes for recruiting women.

People from immigrant backgrounds appear to be an emerging priority for recruiters. Sweden has specific armed forces recruitment programmes targeted at these communities, which are tied in with state unemployment agencies.[22] In the UK, focused recruitment drives among black and minority-ethnic groups had increased their representation among enlisted recruits from 6.1% in 2006 to 7.9% in 2012.[23] However, the proportion of black or minority-ethnic officers remains unchanged at just 2.4%, reflecting the abiding class difference between commanders and commanded.[24] In both groups, the proportion of people from black and minority-ethnic backgrounds is much lower than that in the general proportion, at 14%.[25] Whilst in some countries, such as Sweden, recruits with immigrant backgrounds might be valued positively for their cultural knowledge[26], generally the armed forces capitalise on the socio-economic weakness of minority populations in order to fill the ranks.

Since presenting a more realistic picture of military life would leave recruiters a long way short of their recruitment targets, they have to engage in a propaganda exercise. As one recruiter put it to me: 'You have to tell the truth... to a degree.'[27] Degrees of truth implies degrees of lies or omission. Understanding how recruitment propaganda is constructed helps to inform effective challenges to it. A fundamental weakness of military recruitment is that it has to persuade young people of two things that are not true. The first claim aligns soldiering with civilian society. It says that soldiering is a normal thing to do; it is a career choice no different in kind from being a teacher or a baker; powerful armed forces are needed as part of what makes a society civilised; the lifestyle of a soldier is almost the same as a civilian's anyway. The second claim, paradoxically, elevates soldiers above civilian society. Joining the army automatically makes you special, powerful, more of a person, even a hero.

This pattern is common to European countries relying on 'voluntary' recruitment and which are not involved in military conflict on their own soil. It is also true of Ghana, where being a soldier attracts social status and high pay, and South Africa. It seems to be less the case in the countries represented at the Darmstadt workshop which do not need to market military careers, usually because they rely on conscription, such as Switzerland and Colombia, or where the realities of war are closer to home, such as Colombia.

Responding

Some of the best criticism of this recruitment messaging comes from within armed forces themselves. As General Sir Michael Rose pointed out, soldiering, insofar as it boils down to killing and possibly being killed, is nothing like other jobs. Indeed, it raises searching ethical questions, of which perhaps the most fundamental is 'Can killing be humane?' Personally, I believe that the main challenge for activists is not to persuade young people of a specific view about the rights and wrongs of violence, but to help make sure that these questions are being asked when someone considers signing up. After all, a good choice is not merely a free and informed one, but a responsible one as well.

As for the ubiquitous soldier-hero, this constructed figure is barely recognised by soldiers themselves. I know of no experienced soldier who thinks all soldiers are heroes. Rather, they tend to think this over-used epithet cheapens the genuinely heroic acts of those soldiers who have put themselves at mortal risk for the sake of their comrades. The soldier-hero is a civilian concoction actively encouraged by politicians and the media, which tacitly encourages us to believe (or not to question) that the wars fought in other countries in our name must be noble and necessary. The reality is that many soldiers who have seen the brute horror and political calamity of wars think politicians, who have seen a lot less, are far too ready to start them.[28]

Military recruitment is deeply embedded in the class and economic structures of society. Its methods, thriving on hyper-masculine fantasies of soldiering and, in consumer-capitalist societies in particular, a creeping estrangement from our most humane values, can be understood as a form of human alienation. Even so, despite the continuing success of military recruitment worldwide, it is still perhaps the Achilles heel of militarism. War depends on large numbers of people agreeing to participate in mass killing. If we can work well with young people, their parents, educators and the media, so that equally large numbers pause to reflect on what soldiers are expected to do and why, cracks might open in militarism from the bottom up.

Notes

1 The title paraphrases a statement by a Committee of the British House of Commons: 'We believe it continues to be important to recruit young people straight from school, including at the age of 16; if they are not caught at this point, they are likely to take up other careers and be permanently lost to the Armed Forces.' House of Commons Select Committee on the Armed Forces Bill, 'Armed Forces: First Special Report' (London, 2001), paragraph 63 [Online at www.publications.parliament.uk/pa/cm200001/cmselect/cmarmed/154/15403.ht m (accessed 19 April 2013)].
2 Throughout this article, the term 'soldier' is used as shorthand for enlisted personnel in national armies, navies and air forces.
3 Ministry of Defence, *Army Career Guide to Infantry Soldier* (London, 2005).
4 'How soon could our Army lose a war?', *The Daily Telegraph*, 5 April 1998, cited in British Parliament, House of Commons Defence Committee, 'Duty of Care', 1:28 (2005).
5 Human Rights Act 1998, Art. IV
6 Ibid., Ch. 3.1.
7 David Gee and Anna Goodman, 'Army recruiters visit London's poorest schools most often' (2010) [Online at www.informedchoice.org.uk/armyvisitstoschools.pdf (accessed 18 April 2013)].
8 David Gee, 'Informed Choice? Armed forces recruitment practice in the United Kingdom' (London, 2008), Ch. 4.1 [Online at www.informedchoice.org.uk/informedchoice/informedc hoiceweb.pdf (accessed 16 May 2013)].
9 Khalida Ismail et al, 'Occupational risk factors for ill health in Gulf veterans of the United Kingdom', *Journal of Epidemiological and Community Health*, 54 (2000), pp. 834-8; Nicola Fear et al, 'What are the consequences of deployment to Iraq and Afghanistan on the

mental health of the UK armed forces? A cohort study', *The Lancet*, 375 (2010), pp. 1783-97; Amy Iversen et al, 'The prevalence of common mental disorders and PTSD in the UK military: using data from a clinical interview-based study', BMC Psychiatry, 9:68 (2009), unpaginated [Online at www.biomedcentral.com/1471-244X/9/68 (accessed 18 April 2013)]; Matthew Hotopf et al, 'The health of UK military personnel who deployed to the 2003 Iraq war: a cohort study', *The Lancet*, 367 (2006), pp. 1731–41; Margaret Jones et al, 'The burden of psychological symptoms in UK Armed Forces', *Occupational Medicine*, 56 (2006), p. 326; Matthew J. Friedman et al, 'Post-traumatic stress disorder in the military veteran', *Psychiatric Clinics of North America*, 17:2 (1994), pp. 265-77.

10 Charles Hoge et al, 'Combat Duty in Iraq and Afghanistan, Mental Health Problems, and Barriers to Care', *The New England Journal of Medicine*, 351:1 (2004), pp. 13-22; Hotopf et al, 'The health of UK military personnel', pp. 1731–41; Jones et al, 'The burden of psychological symptoms', pp. 322-88; Fear et al, 'What are the consequences of deployment to Iraq and Afghanistan', pp. 1783-97; Iversen et al, 'The prevalence of common mental disorders and PTSD in the UK military'; Friedman et al, 'Post-traumatic stress disorder', pp. 265-277; Ismail et al, 'Occupational risk factors for ill health in Gulf veterans', pp. 834-8; Amy Iversen et al, 'Influence of childhood adversity on health among male UK military personnel', *The British Journal of Psychiatry*, 191 (2007), pp. 506-11.

11 Among deployed troops who had experienced no direct combat engagements, the authors found a PTSD rate of 4.5%; among those with experience of five or more direct combat engagements, the rate had risen to 19.3%: Hoge et al, 'Combat Duty in Iraq and Afghanistan', pp. 13-22; Friedman et al, 'Post-traumatic stress disorder', pp. 265-77. It is important to note that someone who causes trauma to others may themselves be traumatised as a result; this so-called 'moral pain' raises questions about the link between mental health problems and unarticulated conscientious objection.

12 Fear et al, 'What are the consequences of deployment to Iraq and Afghanistan', pp. 1783-97; Iversen et al, 'The prevalence of common mental disorders and PTSD in the UK military'; Ismail et al, 'Occupational risk factors for ill health in Gulf veterans', pp. 834-8; Jones et al, 'The burden of psychological symptoms', pp. 322-88; Iversen et al, 'Influence of childhood adversity on health among male UK military personnel', pp. 506-11; Friedman et al, 'Post-traumatic stress disorder', pp. 265-77.

13 David Gee and Anna Goodman, 'Youngest recruits face greatest risks in Afghanistan' (London, 2013) [forthcoming – please contact the author].

14 Calculated from Ministry of Defence, 'British Fatalities: Operations in Afghanistan' (2013) [Online at www.gov.uk/government/fields-of-operation/afghanistan (accessed 13 March 2013)].

15 Child Soldiers International and ForcesWatch, 'One Step Forward: The case for ending the recruitment of minors by the British armed forces' (London, 2013).

16 Coalition to Stop the Use of Child Soldiers [now called Child Soldiers International], 'Catch 16-22: Recruitment and retention of minors in the British armed forces' (London, 2011), pp. 9-10 [Online at www.child-soldiers.org/research_report_reader.php?id=290 (accessed 18 April 2013)]; Sarah Rutherford et al, 'Quantitative & Qualitative Research into Sexual Harassment in the Armed Forces' (Equal Opportunities Commission and the Ministry of Defence, 2006).

17 Ismail et al, 'Occupational risk factors for ill health in Gulf veterans', pp. 834-8.

18 Iversen et al, 'The prevalence of common mental disorders and PTSD in the UK military'.

19 Sally McManus et al (eds), 'Adult psychiatric morbidity in England, 2007: Results of a household survey' (National Health Service, 2009) [Online at www.ic.nhs.uk/pubs/psychiatricmorbidity07 (accessed 13 May 2010)].

20 Ibid.

21 Colombia, Holland, Germany, Ghana, South Africa, Spain, Sweden, Switzerland, UK.

22 Swedish activist, personal communication, 14 April 2013.

23 Defence Analytical Services and Advice, 'Strength of UK Regular Forces by Service and ethnic origin, at 1 April each year' [Online at www.dasa.mod.uk (accessed 6 January 2013)].

24 Ibid.
25 Office for National Statistics, 'Ethnicity and National Identity in England and Wales 2011' [Online at www.ons.gov.uk/ons/dcp171776_290558.pdf (accessed 6 January 2013)].
26 Swedish activist, personal communication, 14 April 2013.
27 Recruiting staff, London, personal communication, November 2007.
28 See for example Ken Lukowiak, *A Soldier's Song* (London, 1993); Lee Jones, *Nobody's Hero: A Reluctant March Through the Middle East* (Oxford, 2007).

The militarisation of everyday life in Venezuela

Rafael Uzcátegui

The recently-deceased President Hugo Chavez systematically militarised Venezuelan society, from young to old. This is perhaps not too surprising when recalling that he came to power as Lieutenant Colonel Chavez in 1998, after leading a coup d'etat in 1992. It was the first time during the democratic period, which began in 1958, that a member of the armed forces was chosen as the country's leader. Since that time there has been a progressive militarisation of the country, with a special emphasis on young people.

This article considers the concept of militarisation in a broad sense, not just as the physical presence of soldiers in the daily life of the population. Militarisation is the spreading of and granting privilege to the values, symbols, language and ways of thinking and acting used by the armed forces within society, in order to guarantee the government's ability to govern.

Starting them young

In 1981 'pre-military instruction' was added as an optional subject to the curriculum of the last two years of secondary education in public schools, prior to university. It became mandatory in both public and private education in 1999. Theoretical classes about the origins of the state and the nation from a military perspective are mixed with practical military drill, exercises in survival and military confrontation, such as describing the weapons used by the military. Sometimes putting together and dismantling a pistol can also be part of the course. One part gives an historical overview of the establishment of Venezuela as a country that has won successive military victories against different empires, i.e. history told from a military perspective, whilst another part gives classes about human rights...

The Bolivarian government has created new higher education institutions, such as the Bolivian University of Venezuela (UBE) and the National University of the Arts (UNEARTE) and their disciplinary rules look more like those of a barracks than a university. At UBE student unions are prohibited, while at UNEARTE much behaviour is classified as lack of respect for authority and punished with expulsion.

An old university exclusively for the military today forms part of the system of public universities: the National Experimental Polytechnic University of the Armed Forces (UNEFA), where enrolment has grown significantly since 2004, from 2,500 students to 230,000. The students receive a militarised education with different rituals, which are more appropriate on a military base, such as singing the national anthem before classes. UNEFA prides itself on actively contributing to the training of the National Bolivarian Military, a civil component of the Armed Forces created by Chavez's administration. According to official figures, this 'civilian' military is made up of 13,000 men and women from all over the country. University authorities claim that students join the military voluntarily, but it is not clear if they can graduate if they refuse to participate.

The Bolivarian National Military uses article 326 of the Constitution as a presumed source of legitimacy. This article talks of the 'principle joint responsibility of citizens in the integral defence of the nation.' Up until now, this interpretation has created three types of civil-military undertakings: the Territorial Military, the military reserve, and the combatant corps. The difference between the military and the combatant corps is that the latter, according to the Partial Reform of the Statutory law of the National Bolivarian Armed Forces, approved in 2009, must be organised in public and private companies, 'to ensure the integrity and operation of the institutions where they came from.' President Chavez's government programme of 2013-2019 promised in point 1.1.3.3 'to expand the organisation of towns for the integral defence of the country', which portends the continual, profound militarisation of society.

The combatant corps don't have anything to do with the educative model driven by the so-called 'Bolivarian revolution': spokespersons from institutions such as the Romula Gallegos University (Unerg), Simon Rodrigues University (USR) and the National Open University (UNA) - old institutions of superior education but which are now openly controlled by the government - have affirmed their commitment to organise them [the corps] from the inside, with their workers. A similar commitment with the reinforcement of the military can also be found in the Bolivarian University of Venezuela (UBV). Publicity designed to attract young people to join the reserves can be found in universities. The student movement that supported president Chávez was very supportive of this, setting up their own units. Until now there has not been a clear, natural link between education institutions and the military, and the initiatives are isolated efforts with little coordination between each other. Nevertheless, evidence shows a desire to advance towards greater coordination, creating institutionality for the 'integral defence' of the nation which has the education system as one of its components.

Another military initiative has been the creation, by the State, of so-called 'communicational guerilla commandos' which, paradoxically, came from the female leader of government of the Capital District, Jacqueline Faría, in April 2010. The project was to involve units of 25 young students with an average education to face what the government calls the 'communicational supremacy' of private media. The adolescents swore an oath in front of patriotic symbols, dressed in the military style of Latin American guerrillas from the 1960's, and were supplied with different tools to make street murals. However, this initiative did not prosper: different human rights and social organisations questioned its legitimisation of armed violence.

Another example of militarism meddling with young Venezuelan minds is the use of symbolic elements which suggest that the vertical and authoritarian model represented by the Armed Forces is the most efficient model for organising one's life in society. Despite the civil vote of confidence in him, President Chavez became accustomed to attending official ceremonies in military uniform. The red beret, used by leaders of coup d'états and by Chavez himself, during February 1992, formed an important part of Bolivarian dress. The Paseo de Los Proceres in Caracas - a military infrastructure inaugurated in 1956 by the dictator Marcos Perez Jimenez - remains a privileged site for its military marches as well as its public demonstrations in support of the government, for example, the inaugural march of the 6th Global Social Forum, which took place there in January 2006.

Not just the youth: History, violence, and space

The militarisation of youth in Venezuela is part of the general militarisation of the country and therefore needs to be put into context. Following the general tendency of Latin American countries, Venezuela is a country whose history is a succession of wars and military heroes. Of these heroes, Simon Bolivar is the towering figure, having won independence from Spain for Bolivia, Colombia, Ecuador, Panama, Peru and Venezuela. Four years after his death in 1830, the Venezuelan Congress began to institutionalise homage to him, honouring him with the title The Liberator. In 1880, President Guzman Blanco named the Venezuelan currency as Bolivar and ordered statues of him to be put up in every city's main square. Today, all Venezuelan cities and towns have a statue or bust of Bolivar in their centres. He was said to have a 'warlike' or 'warrior's' masculinity and is the model for Venezuelan men, with emphasis on maleness, valour, and patriotism. Venezuelan masculinity is a projection of the figure of Bolívar. Chávez reinforced this: despite being a 'civilian' president he always carried out public acts in military dress and in all his analysis and description of political conflict he employed military metaphors. Public functionaries and his supporters called him Commander-President, public bodies were given names such as Organisation of Electoral Battle, and Combatant Corps, and the majority of slogans contained military allusions, such as 'Order over this front'.

Throughout Latin America, Bolivar's figure and thoughts have been used to give legitimacy to political movements from both the Left and the Right. Juan Vicente Gomez's dictatorship in Venezuela between 1908 and 1935 was an active promoter of paying homage to Simon Bolivar's persona. People wrongly believe that the current Venezuelan army descends from Simon Bolivar's liberation army, but Bolívar's army only lasted until 1870; it wasn't until the 1930s that the modern Venezuelan army was created, by Gómez. From 1958 onwards, the different democratic governments called upon the Bolivarian legend in different ways. Chavez did the same. His insurrectionist movement after 1992 was called The Bolivarian Revolutionary Movement 200. After rising to power in 1998 through the democratic route, the new government changed the country's name to the Bolivarian Republic of Venezuela. Chavez's own political movement is called the Bolivarian Revolution.

A new Constitution was written in 1999. One of the changes was the inclusion for the first time of military personnel's right to vote. It also granted them other political rights, such the right to be elected to public office. Today, soldiers are ministers, governors and mayors. Although there is a coalition of political parties that supported President Chavez - the Great Patriotic Pole - there is a lot of evidence that, in fact, the Armed Forces are Hugo Chavez's political organisation, trusted with exercising political power. We can see an example of this in the governor's elections on 16 December 2012, where the United Socialists Party of Venezuela (PSUV) nominated candidates to twenty-three state governments of the country, twelve of whom were in the military. Of these, eleven were elected.

In Venezuela there is a primacy of violence – symbolic or real – as a means of resolving conflicts. Victory is understood as the elimination or humiliation of the other. Venezuela has one of the highest homicide rates in the region. Historically, management posts within the country's police force are given to military personnel, and the police use military weaponry. Security operations, including the recent 'Bicentennial Security Plan', count heavily on the Bolivarian National Guard (GNB), which is one of the four components making up the Bolivarian National Armed Forces (FANB). Between 1997 and 2011, according to figures from the human rights charity Provea, the Armed Forces – especially the GNB - were responsible for 301 cases regarding the violation of the right to live. The human rights coalition 'Foro por la Vida' (Forum For Life) has demanded of the government to 'guarantee that, except for in exceptional circumstances, the Armed Forces do not participate in civil security activities.' The GNB is also in charge of guarding the country's prisons, where according to data in 2011 from the Venezuelan Prison Observatory (OVP), there were 560 deaths and 1,457 injuries in the country's 35 prisons. The GNB is accused of controlling the weapons and drugs traffic in the prisons.

The serious violence in Venezuela has been categorised as a 'low intensity war' by different experts. Keeping oneself 'safe' has engendered an important change in habits and customs. These include, among others; recreation, cultural activities and the loss of public areas in the country's main cities. In the city centre of the country's capital, Caracas, commercial activities stop at 6pm for security reasons, and in other main cities public transport services are progressively limited. People stay in their homes at night. Young people tend to gather in large shopping centres.

Another aspect of the militarisation of young people is the strategies rolled out to control social conflicts, which reproduce the Armed Forces' own war logic. Since 2002, after the approval of the Constitutional Law of National Security, 'security zones' were created in Venezuela: 'spaces (...) subject to special regulation.' According to the law, security zones are:

- the shores, lakes, islands and navigable rivers
- oil and gas pipelines, aqueducts and main electricity lines
- areas surrounding military and public facilities, basic and strategic industries, and essential services
- the airspace above military facilities, basic and strategic industries, and essential services
- the most important adjacent areas of air, ground and water communication channels
- any other security zone considered necessary for the nation's security and defence.

According to calculations by the charity Control Ciudadano (Citizen Control), almost 30% of Venezuela would be considered a security zone. According to article 56 of the law, 'Anyone who organises, supports or instigates the carrying out of activities within security zones which are intended to disturb or affect the organisation and functioning of military facilities, public services, industries and basic companies, or the socio-economic life of the country, will be punished with a 5-10 year prison sentence. The supposed crime of 'violation of security zones' is commonly used to criminalise popular social leaders for staging peaceful protests in the country. In 2011 the human rights charity Provea condemned the existence of 2,400 cases of people brought to court for participating in a protest. Most of these people were young rural leaders, union members, or students. However, the security zones law is not the only means of territorial control of political rights. Multiple areas and spaces of the country are considered 'Bolivarian territory' where activities and the expression of any other political views are prohibited. In 1999 in Bolivar state, a frontier state bordering on Brazil, the Pemón people brought down twelve electrical pylons that were part of a power line project between Venezuela and Brazil that passed through indigenous territories in Venezuela. As a result the area was militarised through the presence of the armed forces and the landmines that they planted around other electrical pylons to prevent them being brought down.

Several urban and rural paramilitary organisations in the country support the government and have young people among their members. Human rights organisations have denounced Colombian groups such as the FARC and ELN, and the Venezuelan Bolivarian Forces of Liberation (FBL), for practising the forced recruitment of adolescents at the Venezuelan border. The Constitution of 1999 recognises the right to conscientious objection in an ambiguous way. Because of the lack of employment and other opportunities, military service constitutes a source of employment and social ascent for young people from the poorer sectors of society. According to the budget for the Armed Forces, they will receive 15[6] times more money than they can earn as particants on the Ministry of Youth programmes, which are aimed at benefitting young people in Venezuela.

Translated from the original Spanish by Paul Rankin

Publicity campaigns: The German Armed Forces' struggle for the hearts and minds of the population

Michael Schulze von Glaßer

Small and ready to fight. In spite of a general reduction in personnel, the German Bundeswehr (Armed Forces) should in the future be more fit for action: 10,000 German soldiers should be able to be deployed abroad at any time, instead of the current 7,000.[1] But since the suspension of conscription, the Armed Forces have to meet their recruitment needs entirely by persuading volunteers to join up: 170,000 career soldiers, soldiers on contract, and reservists, plus up to 15,000 people doing voluntary military service. This calculation was presented by Minister of Defence Thomas de Maizière (Christian Democrats) in a policy speech in Berlin on 18 June 2011. At present, it does not seem to be a problem for the Armed Forces to find the 5,000 new recruits required every year. In the first year they were able to enlist 12,461 soldiers for voluntary military service.[2] However, one quarter of these left the Armed Forces shortly afterwards, leaving 9,400 new recruits. This number is, at least in the long run, probably too low.

But there is also another reason for the increasing public presence of the Armed Forces, articulated by the former president Horst Köhler (Christian Democrats) in an oft-quoted speech at the Armed Forces Commanders Conference in Bonn in 2005: 'The Germans trust their Armed Forces, and rightfully so, but real interest or even pride in it are rather rare. Even more rare is the wish and an attempt to understand and assess the changed foreign and security policy, which is impacting the German Bundeswehr. Of course we can name reasons for this friendly disinterest'.[3] Among the reasons for this 'friendly disinterest', Köhler cited the experience of World War II and the lack of a sense of threat. However, besides disinterest there is a stable majority within Germany which views German military operations abroad critically. For example, about 60% to 70% of the German population have opposed the deployment of the Armed Forces in Afghanistan for years and have demanded a fast withdrawal of German troops.[4] This means that whenever the German military presents itself in public, the polishing of its public image is a priority, so that in the future, they can go to war not just with the support of the German parliament, but also with the support of the German people.

In city centres

In 2006, acting on advice from the Bundeswehr Institute of Social Sciences, the Armed Forces created a new promotional unit called The Central Fairs and Event Marketing Department of the Armed Forces. Since then, they have been promoting

35

enlistment as 'a career with a future.'[5] The flagship of this promotional unit is the so-called Career Meeting Point (KarriereTreff), consisting of three large trucks – the career truck, the cinema truck, and the equipment truck. These trucks tour all over Germany all year round visiting about forty cities, where they position themselves prominently in central places or at public events. The second tool of the unit is a large booth for fairs, which is used about fifty times every year, including at Gamescom, Europe's largest video games fair, and at medical congresses, where it attempts to counteract its massive shortfall of medical personnel.

In addition to the Central Fairs and Event Marketing unit, all four regional military commands (North, East, South, and West) have their own Armed Forces Centres for Recruitment. Each of these units has two booths for fairs - similar to but smaller than that of Central Fairs and Event Marketing - and four smaller promotion trucks, which are used for career advice and the distribution of brochures. At almost all of the promotional events there are also military vehicles and equipment, such as tanks and helicopters.

Children climbing on a tank at a military open day in Niederstetten, September 2011
(credit - Michael Schulze von Glaßer)

Military ceremonies

The number of public military oath ceremonies outside military barracks has recently increased, especially under the leadership of former Minister of Defence Franz Josef Jung (Christian Democrats): there were 180 in 2009, as opposed to the 134 in 2007.[6] In 2008, the large military oath ceremony which is part of the annual public remembrance day for the attempted assassination of Adolf Hitler on 20 July 1944, was for the first time moved from the Bendlerblock (the Berlin seat of the Ministry of Defence) to the Reichstag, the German parliament.[7] In recent years, these ceremonies were transmitted live by the public TV broadcaster Phoenix.[8] Because the suspension of conscription also means a reduction in the number of new recruits, it is to be expected that the overall number of such ceremonies will go down – whether this reduction also includes public oath ceremonies, or only those held in military barracks, is currently unclear.

In addition, there are numerous traditional major military ceremonies (so-called 'grand tattoos'), which mark events such as a President or Minister of Defence standing down, which also might be shown live on television. In 2006 there were twenty, and in 2010 there were seven. More recently, the increasingly elaborate memorial services for soldiers killed in action are sometimes broadcast live by public TV channels, and the first award of the Armed Forces cross for a bravery medal in 2009 is a further indication of this establishment of a new cult of soldiering and heroism.[9] Shortly after the creation of the medal for bravery, a new Bundeswehr cenotaph was opened in Berlin, paying tribute to dead soldiers. Additionally, the eighteen Armed Forces bands, which together perform more than 3,000 concerts annually, play an important role in the promotion of a positive image for the military.

A dead soldier's funeral service is transmitted live on a big public screen in Detmold, June 2011 (credit - Michael Schulze von Glaßer)

Advertising in the media

The Armed Forces spent €15 million from 2006 to 2009 on advertising in the print media, on the radio and in cinemas.[10] Between 2009 and 2011, the expenses for recruitment-related advertising alone have risen to more than €5.7 million per year. The Armed Forces regularly advertise in Germany's largest school magazine, the Spiesser, with a circulation of more than one million.[11] In addition, their radio and cinema advertising targets young people, and focuses especially on recruiting new helicopter and fighter jet pilots. Finally, in spring 2010 and 2011, for the first time in years, they used television advertising. The twenty-second-long advertisement, which cost €189,000, directly promoted the use of weapon systems for: 'Mastering challenges, proving team spirit, mastering technology. Armed Forces – a career with a future', and later also with the slogan 'Armed Forces reform – Your opportunity'.[12] Presently there are two Armed Forces television advertisements, with the new promotional slogan: 'We. Serve. Germany.'

Militainment (military entertainment)

To improve its image even further, the Armed Forces also increasingly subsidise German film production: eleven in 2005, four in 2006, eight in 2007, twelve in 2008, and a record of twenty-two in 2009.[13] They provide film producers with large military equipment, the permission to film on military facilities, and even financial support. They especially support films, TV series, and documentaries which present them in a positive light.

In addition, the Armed Forces is increasingly involved in video games, possibly because it receives more international attention due to its operations abroad. Although as of yet they have only published a handful of browser-based games for recruitment purposes, neither they nor the Ministry of Defence object to their frequent portrayal in video games: indeed, the promotional effect is appreciated.

Conclusions and perspectives

The Armed Force's presence in public spaces has grown markedly in recent years. Advertising in the media in particular should, according to the Ministry of Defence, be increased massively. In 2010, the Armed Forces opened their first recruitment office in the Saarbrücken central railway station, which could be seen as an attempt to be permanently present in the centres of large cities. Since the suspension of conscription, the district conscription boards are to be replaced by 'career centres' and 'career offices', but how this is going to be done – whether the present district conscription boards will also include a promotion and information unit, or whether they will be closed and promotional offices will be opened in city centres instead – is not yet known.[14] As long as the German government continues with an expansionist military policy undertaking global military operations, the promotion of the military on the 'home front' will increase too, until a sufficient number of soldiers are recruited and the German population has been made to accept war.

Notes

1 Süddeutsche Zeitung, 'De Maizière erläutert Bundeswehrreform – Weniger Soldaten aber dafür mehr im Ausland', 27 May 2011. <http://www.sueddeutsche.de/politik/de-maizire-erlaeutert-bundeswehrreform-hauptsache-kein-guttenberg-1.1102283> (accessed 23 August 2012).
2 Süddeutsche Zeitung, 'Aktuelle Vorabmeldung: Soldatenüberschuss: die Bundeswehr ist für junge Leute attraktiver als man denkt', 5 July 2012. <www.sueddeutsche.de> (accessed 23 August 2012).
3 Horst Köhler, 'Einsatz für Freiheit und Sicherheit', Rede von Bundespräsident Horst Köhler auf der Kommandeurtagung der Bundewehr, Bonn, 10 October 2005.
4 Informationsstelle Militarisierung, 'IMI-Fact-Sheet Afghanistan: Das Drama in Zahlen', 28 October 2011. <www.imi-online.de> (accessed 23 August 2012).
5 Michael Schulze von Glaßer, An der Heimatfront – Öffentlichkeitsarbeit und Nachwuchswerbung der Bundeswehr (Cologne, 2010).
6 Bundestags-Drucksache 17/715.
7 Andreas Müller, 'Feierliches Gelöbnis vor historischer Kulisse, 20 July 2008. <www.bmvg.de> (accessed 23 August 2012).
8 Schulze von Glaßer, An der Heimatfront.
9 Bundeswehr, 'Allgemeines: Die Ehrenzeichen der Bundeswehr', 10 January 2012. <www.bundeswehr.de> (accessed 23 August 2012).
10 Bundestags-Drucksache 16/14094.
11 Michael Schulze von Glaßer, 'Armee umwirbt Kinder', 10 May 2009. <www.telepolis.de> (accessed 23 August 2012).
12 Schulze von Glaßer, An der Heimatfront.
13 Bundestags-Druche 16/14094.
14 Michael Schulze von Glaßer, 'Keine "Wehrpflicht", dafür Karrierecenter', 5 December 2011. <www.graswurzel.net> (accessed 23 August 2012).

Translated from the original German by Richard Meakin

Invisible militarism in Israel

Ruti Kantor and Diana Dolev

Background

Militarism is strongly embedded in Israeli society and the education system is, from a very early age, a powerful agent for it. The central place of the army in each Jewish individual's life is demonstrated daily: some people customarily congratulate parents on the birth of a new boy with: 'Mazal Tov! a new soldier is born!' Every kindergarten and school marks and praises military victories and conducts ceremonies in memory of fallen soldiers. Fathers and older brothers of the children, who may themselves be soldiers, often take part in these ceremonies. Children are exposed to tanks, fighter planes and various kinds of weaponry as part of their education and daily routine.

Referring to the concept of militarisation in the context of education in Israel, education researcher and former New Profile activist Haggith Gor wrote in The Militarisation of Education (2005):

> Militarism is a system of values and beliefs that views the use of military force as a suitable means of solving political problems and obtaining political power...Militarisation is the spreading of militarism as ideology and the strengthening of the influence the military has as a social institution. Militarisation processes create a social climate that prepares civilians to accepting war, they create an atmosphere in which the central status of the military appears natural and military solutions to political problems appear reasonable. Militarisation processes happen step by step...Militarisation creeps into people's daily routine.[1]

The presence of the military and militarism in public space is Israel is so much part of our daily routine, so close to us, that we do not see them for what they really are. Unless we develop an awareness of their various appearances we cannot recognise the messages of violence and war that they carry. Thus militaristic messages become normalised and harmless. Or rather, they become an important component of our identity. It is the government education system that acts as a key agent in creating this identity; young people are particularly exposed to this visual militarism, and they are probably even more susceptible to it – even less likely to reflect critically about it – than adults. However, through counter-education we can reverse this militarisation, creating minds that are capable of seeing things critically for what they really are. This article explores some examples of militarisation of Israeli public space, and describes daily responses to them.

Examples

Our civilian environment contains many military images, including armed and uniformed soldiers and military vehicles (both on and off duty), which our children encounter very frequently. Are we really aware of their presence and the consequences?

We can all identify some military and militaristic images, even when they appear in advertisements and computer games. Yet we are unaware of some very conspicuous military and militaristic images in civilian public spaces. Their militaristic nature seems to become concealed, invisible. Perhaps from repeated exposure we have actually trained ourselves to overlook the appearance of militarism in a civilian environment.

Among militarised spaces in Israel, those that are not recognised as such by the general public include, to give just a few typical examples, an art gallery placed in a military memorial hall, a cartoon figure from an advertisement for a lottery wearing a military identification tag, and an old cannon in a public park next to a playground.

Most Israelis, seeing combat soldiers at a bus station, will probably think about the hardships of combat service, and feel sympathy and pride
(credit – Esti Tsal)

Militarised Parenting: Three generations share the joy of this child's possible future (Weapons Expo, Israel, 2008) (credit – Activestills)

Wherever you go in Israel, you are likely to come across soldiers, often carrying guns. It is a fact of everyday life (credit – Esti Tsal)

A decommissioned piece of artillery in a public park next to a playground (credit – Diana Dolev)

Militarism's layers of visibility

Militarism has different layers of visibility. The first one is the highly visible layer, which we can all easily identify: an army base, a tank, a military uniform, a soldier. The second is the semi-concealed, less obvious layer, like popular military video games. The third consists of invisible or hidden militarism, such as the symbolic military tags that people in Israel wear to commemorate dead soldiers. Becoming aware of militaristic messages can be the result of developing an anti-militarist point of view, as this provides a critical lens through which to observe the world.

In the centre of the town of Binyamina, next to the municipal building and the central synagogue, there is a park. National and local public celebrations take place there, and children go to the park with their families on a daily basis. In this park a memorial wall for dead soldiers has been constructed next to a memorial monument for Holocaust victims.

From a young age, Jewish children in Israel are taught to believe that Jews are

Fallen Soldiers Memorial next to the Holocaust memorial Wall, Binyamina (credit – Diana Dolev)

always under existential threat, and that the solution is to maintain a strong military and be prepared to die for Israel. The two adjacent memorials in the Binyamina park, as well as the proximity between Israel's Holocaust Memorial Day, the memorial day for Israeli war casualties and Israel's Independence Day (all three taking place within eight days), are powerful means for reinforcing this message. This raises various questions: how should we train ourselves to actually see and be conscious of invisible militarism in our civil environment? What direct action should we take in order to raise awareness and to avoid concealing the militaristic message in different phenomena?

There are many ways in which we can take action. Often this means improving our own ability to recognise subtle forms of militarism, as well as educating the non-antimilitarist majority. Ideas include:

- producing a photographic exhibition, or film, that documents the different layers of visibility of militarism in your country, and sharing it online
- doing street theatre in response to military propaganda (perhaps highlighting the physical and mental injuries that war causes to both soldiers and civilians)
- holding alternative mirroring events such as the sale and promotion of white peace poppies (instead of the red Remembrance poppies, now inextricably linked to the current armed forces and the pressure to be supportive of them) in the UK
- placing peace symbols such as the rainbow flag and broken rifle badges in as many visible locations as possible

Sharing experiences and ideas of documenting and countering militarism and its symbols will help us to build the necessary awareness to 'read' our militaristic environments. Together we can unveil the less-visible forms of militarism. This will lead to a greater consciousness of the militarisation of society, which should bring about positive and effective responses, such as protests against the presence of weapons as glorifying monuments in public spaces (and especially in children's playgrounds), and lobbying the Ministry of Defence to separate itself from school curricula. In order to do this, we must identify the reasons for our lack of awareness and the danger that this carries when the military is a normal component of the civilian environment. We need to look especially at the impact of this phenomenon on young people, and explore ways to challenge it and to realise alternative, demilitarised public space and symbology.

Notes

1   Haggith Gor (ed.), *The Militarization of Education* (Tel-Aviv, 2005), p. 10.

Monuments and memory in Former Yugoslavia

Boro Kitanoski

I was born in 1976. One of the first memories I have is the anniversary of the death of Josip Broz Tito, Yugoslavia's long serving marshal, World War II hero and life-long president. It was 4 May 1981. Every year after his death, the anniversary was observed by loud sirens in all of the bigger towns in the country, announcing the full stop of all activities for a minute or so: factories, traffic, people on the streets. I remember that I had come out of the house with a handful of biscuits when the siren sounded and everything stopped. All of the other kids and adults on the street stood still. I also stood still, but the cookies in my hand were so enticing that I just had to eat them at that very moment. I couldn't wait till the siren stopped. I remember standing absolutely still, only moving one hand to eat them. I still remember feeling that I had betrayed something and a minute after the sirens stopped, running to my uncle's house and confessing what I had just done. Of course he laughed and comforted me, but he also was proud of me showing such respect to the dead leader.

I live in a highly militarised society. I recognise it in the mindset of people and in their relationships: families are militarised, our education and the way institutions function are militarised. Even our approach to peace is militarised (peace studies in Macedonia are under the College for Defence – formerly Peoples' Defence Studies). Peace is a defence strategy while you are weaker - we often joke about it.

I live in a building with a big underground bomb shelter just across the street. All of the neighboring buildings have bomb shelters. In fact, just a few years ago it was a legal obligation for people building new houses to allot one room in the basement as a potential bomb shelter, with prescribed dimensions.

Education is militarised

I grew up in a strict and militarised school. Visits to army barracks were frequent and included presentations of weapons. We were taught basic survival techniques during an occupation, the detailed construction of the old M48 rifle (despite it not being in official use any more), and how to treat wounds. Many classes were fed nationalism – patriotism - especially in History classes. The lessons were single perspective, always portraying 'us' as victims of historical processes, being under constant danger from neighbours: 'they proved their aggressive politics towards us many times in the past, surely they will do it again'.

Past wars are celebrated as defensive and glorious. The more distant the war, the more positive people's views on it. However, once we are in a war, it is absolutely necessary for everyone to take part in it.

Lack of discussion on what really happens in war

We talk a lot about wars, but don't really say much. There is no real discussion. Talk is highly emotional, full of stories about heroic behaviour and injustice against us. We don't talk about particular cases; we almost never talk about conflicts from a different perspective. Trying to understand the 'opponent's' perceptions is seen as enemy propaganda. The same people who made or supported the wars of the 1990s are still the most respected and often the most powerful. Young people in the Balkans today don't really have memories of what happened during the wars: they are more easily misguided and recruited to the new nationalist armed forces.

Sport has always been a big thing in the Balkans. Symbolically, the bloody collapse of Yugoslavia was once reenacted in a football match in May 1990 in Zagreb between leading clubs from Croatia and Serbia: huge clashes occurred. Years later we realised that those clashes were not really as spontaneous as they were presented as being, like many other things that followed. Sport stadiums are great public spaces for hints of politics to come. Football fans are extremely nationalistic, mono-ethnic, easy to mobilise, and supported by the state or political parties. Small armies to be.

Recruitment by the military

With a high rate of unemployment in the country, the military is seen as a secure and socially respected profession. There are very few jobs of any kind, so the high level of respect towards soldiers and the feelings of nationalism boost support for those choosing a military career. Interest in joining the armed forces is huge: they don't even have to make commercials. Young people see it as very respectable and socially-desirable career choice.

Memorials

All around the Balkans there are hundreds of new monuments built to mark the tragic events of the recent wars, despite that fact that it is illegal to build them. Just before the Darmstadt conference I was in Sarajevo, Bosnia. My friends from the Centre for Nonviolent Action were starting to research war memorials built since the 1990s. They were studying what the monuments look like, what messages they give, who they speak to, and why. Do these memorials really speak to us? Do they give a clue to what people think about the wars? Here are some examples.

- Many memorials are statues of famous war combatants. They are heavily armed, sometimes with more than one weapon. In the village of Radusha in Macedonia, a statue of a local commander was armed with a pistol and two rifles, standing on top of a real tank that had been destroyed during the war of 2001 and allowed to remain as the base of the memorial.

- In many villages in Macedonia and Kosovo it is common to find new memorials in the local cemeteries where there are lots of graves of fallen soldiers from that village, together with civilians. In many places, even civilian

A huge photo of Adem Jashari, a Kosovo Liberation commander who was killed by the Serbian Police and is considered by many in Kosovo to be a war hero in Kosovo, permanently installed in the monument outside the Youth and Sport Centre, Pristina, Kosovo, 2010 (credit - Ferran Cornellà) casualties are presented with national and military symbols. The message is clear: they all died for the national cause. As the saying goes, 'There are no civilians in war...'

- There is a new monument in central Sarajevo to memorialise the tragic loss of over 1,500 of its children during the siege of the town between 1992 and 1996. At the base of the monument it says: 'In memory of the children killed in besieged Sarajevo'. It can be said that, as part of the town was under the control of Serbian forces and not besieged, the monument sadly excludes some of the 'other' children who also died so tragically in the town.

- A message on a monument in Srebrenica is often seen as controversial in the way it interprets revenge and justice. It says: 'In the Name of God the Most Merciful, the Most Compassionate, We pray to Almighty God, May grievance become hope! May revenge become justice! May mothers' tears become prayers that Srebrenica never happens again to anyone anywhere!'

- Many crosses, fleurs-de-lis, eagles and other national symbols - even churches and mosques - are the new marks of ethnic territory telling the one-sided stories of the recent past. Monuments are there to stay for a long time, and there is a general feeling that in many ways they are just a continuation of the war by other means. What we do about it is still uncertain.

While I was working on this article, the police in southern Serbia demolished an illegal memorial with the names of Albanian victims on it. In turn, an antifascist memorial of World War II in Kosovo, considered to be Serbian, was destroyed. The war narrative goes on...

On-screen warfare

Michael Schulze von Glaßer

US troops march into Iran in 2014, the Russian army occupies half of Europe in 2016, and the USA is conquered by North Korea in 2027 – today's video games tell controversial stories which reach an audience of millions. Here is an overview of military video games and the search for alternatives.

According to an inquiry by the Gfk (Society for Consumer Research) Group, the turnover for video game software in 2010 amounted to €1.86 billion in Germany alone.[1] This was 3% more than the previous year. There are now over 22 million people in Germany playing video games, and military-based games are particularly popular: over one million copies of the first-person shooter Battlefield 3 have been sold since its release in October 2011 (more than 15 million copies have been sold worldwide).[2] The video game industry makes billions and has left Hollywood far behind. However, while films are picked apart by critics in numerous feuilletons, video games hardly attract any attention. When they do, it is mostly due to the violence they portray.[3] And yet video games also often make controversial, and political, statements.

Blockbuster military games

In the aforementioned Battlefield 3, the gamer is a US soldier launching an attack on Iran.[4] The battle is set in the year 2014; there had been a coup in Iran and now Western states are threatened by portable atomic bombs. Since the release of Battlefield 3, the Iranian news agency FARS-News has spoken about an 'open war of media' by the Western world against the Islamic republic.[5] The Iranian government banned the game without hesitation, and went a step further, announcing its intention to release several 'opposing games'. Another very popular first-person shooter is the Call Of Duty: Modern Warfare series. The final part of this trilogy was released in November 2011 and provided the creators with a world record turnover of more than one billion US dollars in its first sixteen days on sale.[6] The games narrate the story of ultranationalists who pull strings in Russia to topple the world into a Third World War. In the year 2016 Russian troops march into Berlin and Paris, and Washington is destroyed in a war which sees nuclear weapons and poison gas deployed. The post-Soviet scenario is staged in an action-packed way. A similarly controversial story is that of Homefront, released in 2011.[7] Following the peaceful reunification of the two Korean states under the regime of Kim Jong-un in 2013, the Greater Korean Republic becomes a new world power and occupies neighbouring states. In 2025 the Koreans attack the USA, which has been weakened by economic crises and the bird flu virus, and immediately either put the population in labour camps, or execute them. In Homefront, the gamer is part of a

49

resistance group that tries to weaken the enemy through guerilla attacks. The game was accompanied by an elaborate advertising campaign and sold over one million copies within five weeks of its release.[8]

The yearly 'gamescom' in Cologne, claims to be the biggest video games fair in the world. In 2012, the number of militaristic games on show was enormous, as it has been in the past.[9] A German game producer promoted his new shooter Warface with a replica US Military-helicopter, which you could enter and try the game out on computers inside. Men dressed as US Elite Soldiers walked between the 270.000 visitors (many of them young). And in another hall the real military - the German Armed Forces - were recruiting young people, with a real tank by their stall. Hardly anyone was bothered by this; some visitors even came dressed in army uniforms holding replica guns. The influence of military video games on young people seems to be working.

A boy posing with mock soldiers at Gamescom video games festival in Cologne, August 2012 (credit - Michael Schulze von Glaßer)

German Armed Forces recruitment at Gamescom in Cologne, August 2012 (credit - Michael Schulze von Glaßer)

Battlefield 3, the Call Of Duty: Modern Warfare series, and Homefront are just three recent examples of video games with militaristic and bellicose themes, which are to a large extent glorified, through discourses of herosim and nationalism. The gamer always belongs to the 'good' side and fights for a supposedly just cause. The characters are well-educated and likeable. The enemies are always bloodthirsty, mysterious and 'evil', with motives that usually remain unclear; the gamer can kill them without feeling remorse. However, video games which attempt to promote peace and expose war's atrocities, rather than glorify it, have also been produced.

A military 'shooter' that questions

'A game that makes you feel bad', the Spiegel Online wrote about the third-person shooter Spec Ops – The Line, released in June 2012.[10] The playing style of the big-seller does not differ from others in its genre; the gamer is still required to shoot countless opponents with a multitude of weapons. What makes the game so noteable, however, is the narrative; the developers were guided by the book Heart Of Darkness, written in 1899 by Joseph Conrad, as well as director Francis Ford Coppola's Vietnam war film Apocalypse Now, which entered cinemas in 1979 and built upon Conrad's themes. In Spec Ops, the gamer is the leader of a three-part

US-reconnaissance troop that, in a fictitious near-future scenario, is despatched to Dubai, which has been destroyed by desert storms.[11] In the city there are merciless skirmishes and shoot-outs involving civilians, CIA agents, and US troops under the command of Colonel Konrad, who is meant to be evacuating people.

The unusual aspect: there is no 'good-bad' formula. During some missions, Colonel Konrad's troops seem to abduct the civilians, during others they help them. Moreover, Konrad's soldiers fight against the CIA. The gamer's troop start off fighting alongside the secret service. However, in doing so they unintentionally eliminate the city's remaining water supplies.

The gamer, with the help of two comrades, then fights his way towards Colonel Konrad's troops whose operations centre is located in a high-rise building in the city. The two comrades die in their pursuit: the streets of the ruined city are lined with countless (and at times decomposing) corpses. It is precisely these images which make Spec Ops such an extraordinary game: in one mission the gamer attacks enemy soldiers with phosphorous grenades, but sees how indiscriminate this weapon is when dozens of burning civilians then crawl towards them. The game's narrative is also very unusual: the gamer eventually learns that Colonel Konrad died some time ago and had suffered from a multiple personality disorder. Instead of successfully carrying out the mission of going to Dubai to observe what is happening and then leaving, the gamer and their two companions are drawn ever- closer to the conflict. The Specs Op gamer justifies their own crimes by what Konrad has done before them. They are faced with multiple moral dilemmas: should they save a group of civilians, or a CIA agent who has crucial intelligence? Ultimately, in the crusade of Spec Ops, the gamer belongs to the bad side – despite the best intentions. Jörg Freidrich, lead 'level designer' in the Spec Ops development studio, explained during an interview that 'We want to prompt the gamer to ask: "Who is actually good here? Me? Who is evil? The other people? Is it so clear-cut?" We want the line to be blurred and to show this to the gamers'.[12] The programmers were able to achieve this. Spec Ops is a challenge to the notion of 'humanitarian military missions'; its chilling and at times unbearable images depict the horror of armed conflict.

Even if Spec Ops shouldn't be regarded as outright anti-war, it does present war in an unprecedented way, and it could be an interesting way of engaging young people with a more critical perspective.

Being a journalist in a virtual war

A real alternative to military shooters is 'newsgames'. One example of this genre is the 2007 game Global Conflicts: Palestine (GCP) produced by the Copenhagen-based company Serious Games Interactive. The gamer is a journalist travelling around the Middle East to conduct research for an article on the conflict between

Israel and Palestine. While doing so the gamer is able to decide whether he or she fully supports one side or will make the reports as neutral as possible. Rune Ottosen, a Norwegian professor of Journalism, addressed the game in great detail in his article 'Computer games: peace journalism vs. war propaganda' in the German periodical Wissenschaft & Frieden (Science & Peace). One thing Ottosen examines is the viability of the concept of 'peace journalism', coined by the Norwegian peace and conflict researcher Johann Galtung. Ottosen's verdict: 'GCP addresses a great number of aspects of the conflict. An important dimension is that GCP attempts to remain impartial and allow the gamer to draw his or her own conclusions. However, the gamer can also choose to be biased and make it onto the front page of the Israeli or Palestinian newspapers with one-sided coverage. Therefore GCP helps people to comprehend how biased journalism influences news content – this is, of course, also highly relevant in the real world of news coverage. It is also an important learning outcome and perhaps the most interesting aspect of GCP.'[13]

Since then there have been further Global Conflict games which have thematised conflicts in Latin America (2008), Africa (2009), and Asia (2009).[14] A similar game currently under development is 'Warco – The News Game'. In Warco, which stands for 'war correspondent', the gamer slips into the role of a female video journalist during an armed revolution in a fictitious African state.[15] No people are shot; only photographs. When, or rather whether, Warco will be released is currently unknown. According to an initial announcement from the developers, the intended release date was 2012 – as of 30 November 2012, no further information had been disclosed.[16]

Newsgames provide a peaceful alternative to well-established military shooters. However, they lack financially-powerful supporters and publishers, and the current journalist games are therefore far behind the best-selling video games on a technical level (graphics, sound, and so on). For many gamers, newsgames simply lack appeal, and the demand remains low – a vicious circle.

Conclusion

Most of today's military video games have a huge impact by spreading messages of acceptable military operations and just wars (of aggression), while also glorifying military practice and   technology. At the same time they create stereotypes of enemies, and make one-sided political statements which can have an impact in the real world. In newsgames there is an alternative, whereby the gamer is confronted with the consequences of war and is shown the advantages of peace. However, such games cannot keep up technically with the major military games, and are currently unpopular. At the moment newsgames remain niche and will not become serious competition for military shooters and other war-related games in the foreseeable future, despite the eager reporting by almost all video game magazines after Warco's announcement, and initial images from it appearing to be highly promising.

Spec Ops – The Line finds a middle ground. The technical aspects of the game manage to keep up with popular military shooters and the structure is similar, but its content which sets it apart: war is not glorified but rather shown for what it is, through atrocious images. There is no 'good-bad' dichotomy and the gamer's main character is ultimately not a hero but rather a broken mass murderer.

Even if, from a pacifist perspective, Spec Ops can only be regarded as a 'reform' of traditional militaristic video games – unlike newsgames it is not 'revolutionary' - more such games would be a good thing, particularly since on a technical level it appeals to the young people who would otherwise play games which glorify war. A newsgame able to keep up with the technical level of popular military video games while offering a well-devised, exciting and interesting narrative whilst also promoting peace, would be indispensable. However, no such game is within sight.

Transparency is needed regarding the military's involvement with video game developers, and public debate on whether this is appropriate should be encouraged. Video games companies producing traditional militaristic video games, and software producers connected to the military - such as those who sell them software for shooting simulators - should be criticised. This could include protesting outside the software companies' headquarters. Critical responses to war-glorifying video games have been lacking within the international peace movement. More energy and resources should be used to develop strategies to campaign against these games.

Notes

1   Bundesverband Interaktiver Unterhaltungssoftware Games Report 2011, 'Zahlen und Fakten zur deutschen Games-Industrie'. <www.biu-online.de> (accessed 24 December 2011).
2   The-Khoa Nguyen, 'Battlefield 3 – Verkaufszahlen in Deutschland – plattformübergreifend über eine Million verkaufte Exemplare', 14 August 2012. <www.pcgames.de> (accessed 22 August 2012); 'Battlefield Inside: Battlefield 3 und Battlefield 3 Premium Verkaufszahlen', 1 August 2012. <www.battlefield-inside.de> (accessed 22 August 2012).
3   Christian Schiffer, 'Machtspiele im digitalen Sandkasten – wie politisch sind Computerspiele?', in Rudolf Thomas Inderst & Peter Just (eds), Contact – Conflict – Combat – Zur Tradition des Konflikts in digitalen Spielen (Boizenburg, 2011), p. 71.
4   Michael Schulze von Glaßer, 'Battlefield 3: Das virtuelle Schalchtfeld', 21 February 2012. <www.imi-online.de> (accessed 23 August 2012).
5   Michael Schulze von Glaßer, 'Krieg der Kriegsspiele', 14 July 2012. <www.telepolis.de> (accessed 23 August 2012).
6   Giga, 'Call of Duty: Modern Warfare 3 – Bringt Activision 1 Millarde Umsatz', 12 December 2011. <www.giga.de> (accessed 23 August 2012).
7   Michael Schulze von Glaßer, 'Die Groß-Koreanische Republik vernichtet die USA', 7

March 2011. <www.telepolis.de> (accessed 23 August 2012).

8   Ali Wenzel, 'Homefront: Schlägt Crysis 2 mit seinen Verkaufszahlen um Längen!', 30 April 2011. <www.pcgames.de> (accessed 23 August 2012).

9   See my Flickr account for photos: www.flickr.com/photos/michaelsvg.

10 Ole Reißmann, 'Spec Ops: The Line – Wahnsinn in der Wüste', 10 July 2012. <www.spiegel.de> (accessed 13 July 2012).

11 Michael Schulze von Glaßer, 'Spec Ops – The Line: Das virtuelle Schlachtfeld', 27 July 2012. <www.imi-online.de> (accessed 22 August 2012).

12 Peter Steinlechner and Michael Wieczorek, 'Spec Ops The Line – Interview und Gameplay', 22 November 2011. <www.golem.de> (accessed 18 Juy 2012).

13 Rune Ottosen, 'Computerspiele als Instrument der Kriegspropaganda? – Bietet Friedensjournalismus eine Alternative?', in Dossier Nr. 69 'Computerspiele: Friedensjournalismus vs. Kriegspropaganda', in *Wissenschaft & Frieden*, 1 (2012).

14 More information on the Serious-Games website: www.globalconflicts.eu

15 Markus Böhm, 'Reporter-Simulation "Warco" – Mit der Kamera durchs Kriegsgebiet', 29 September 2012. <www.spiegel.de> (accessed 30 November 2012).

16 Ibid.

Translated from the original German by Richard Meakin

The impact of internal conflict and the para-state[1] in Colombia

Jorge Vélez

Today in Colombia, it is mostly young men who are sent to fight in the civil war that rages in the most impoverished and vulnerable cities and countryside and which continues to cause widespread deaths and destruction of the land. Sadly, it is a conflict between people who share the same social and economic background. Far right-wing oligarchs perpetuate the war and block dialogue between the parties in conflict. They do this because they are very scared of losing the only enemy that has justified their anti-populist reforms, actions and attacks. In order to understand how this parlous state of affairs has come about and to talk about the militarisation of the country – and in particular its youth - it is necessary to look at its history.

1948 and the conservative strategy of stigmatisation and persecution

The current war in Colombia dates back to 1948, when the presidential candidate Jorge Eliecer Gaitán was murdered and the possibility that socialist ideas would gain a foothold was crushed. Between 1948 and 1953, approximately 300,000 Colombian men and women were murdered in confrontations between the political right and left, in the period known as 'La violencia' (The Violence). It should be made clear that even before this, Liberals and Conservatives had murdered each other in their thousands – there were 14,000 violent deaths in 1947[2], which Gaitán himself condemned in his 1948 speech 'La oración de la paz' (The prayer of peace).

FARC: Origins of the insurgency

FARC (The Revolutionary Armed Forces of Colombia) came into being with the transformation of the Liberal and communist peasant self defence force into structured guerrilla units whose aim was to get into power. The bombardment carried out by the government against a group of peasants in Marquetalia on 27 May 1964 inevitably transformed the conflict that had already been going on between the Colombian state and the armed peasants in the south of Tolima, following the disbandments and amnesties carried out by dictator General Gustavo Rojas Pinilla in 1953. Forty-eight fighters resisted the attacks of that bombardment.[3] Later, 'the self-defence unit became mobile guerrillas through the creation of the so-called Southern Front in 1964. Two years later, it became the

Revolutionary Armed Forces of Colombia (FARC)'.[4]

For FARC, the political and military project remains: it is faced with a context of inequality, persecution and pillage which led to its creation in the 60s. However, the current political, military and social situation in Colombia resulting from the damage caused by the war - so long and destructive that it has dampened any hopes for change through military means - requires a negotiated exit.

The state strategy of working with right-wing paramilitaries in defence of political and economic privileges

The origin of the armed forces of the extreme right dates back to the middle of the twentieth century, with the chulavita and pajaros 'police'[5] - private gangs formed from armed police units and supported by the state, who murdered 'liberal peasants in several of the country's rural regions'.[6] Key developments in the subsequent history of state-supported paramilitarism include: the 1968 Law 48, which authorised the supply of weapons to civilians to fight against the insurgency; the training provided by the US military in creating private anti-terrorist and anti-communist armed groups in the 1970s; the 1981 creation of 'Death to Kidnappers' (MAS) by drug traffickers and the Colombian military, and of 'social cleansing' groups - like the Twelve Apostles in Yarumal, Antioquia - at the end of that decade; the formal founding of the right-wing United Self-Defence Forces of Colombia (AUC) in 1997; the Pact of Ralito signed in 2001 by the main paramilitary bosses and recognised by the different political factions; funding of Álvaro Uribe Vélez's campaign for the presidency in 2002 by paramilitary groups; the removal of FARC by the armed forces, police, and AUC from Medellín in Operation Orion in October 2002; and President Álvaro Uribe Vélez's (2002-10) creation of the Network of Volunteers, which was joined by disbanded paramilitaries. All of these groups and initiatives were created in order to defend the privileges of the liberal and conservative oligarch class of landowners and aristocrats. As the politician Gustavo Petro commented in the debate on the origins of paramilitarism in Antioquia: 'paramilitarism didn't arise because the State didn't exist – it arose alongside sectors of the State'.

War in figures: Investment in Defence and Security, and the size of the various armed forces

The state investment in defence and security – activities and services of National Defence - was 9.954 trillion pesos in 2012, and in Public Order and Citizen Security was 9.759 trillion; both equating to 3% of GDP. In comparison, 2% of GDP was spent on healthcare, 2.9% on education, and 0.3% on housing.[7] It is estimated that funding for guerrilla operations in 2004 were 1.697 trillion pesos for FARC and 743 billion pesos for the National Liberation Army (ELN).[8]

In 2010 the Colombian Army, Air Force and Navy had 284,724 personnel, and the armed National Police had 153,231 officers. As for guerrillas, according to state figures FARC has between 8,500 and 9,000 members, and ELN has between 2,000 and 2,200. There are no accurate figures for the right-wing paramilitaries, though nearly 32,000 members were disbanded after 2003, many remaining active but referred to by the state as BACRIM (criminal bands) to give the impression in public and official discourse that paramilitarism had been dismantled. According to one estimate these bands comprised between 7,100 and 14,500 members in 2010 (depending on whether support networks are included).[9] Attacks against defenders of human rights diminished from 2004 to 2007 - coinciding with the disbanding process -and significantly increased from 2008 'which would seem to be a response to the creation and expansion of criminal gangs spawned from paramilitarism'.[10]

The current situation: fear, violence and armed social control in Medellín

The ongoing social and armed conflict in Colombia intensifies and radicalises militarisation, in terms of the level of violence, the way the media portrays it, and the heavy recruitment – particularly of poor young men - by both sides.

In Medellín and Antioquia, the forced recruitment by the state Armed Forces in public transport stations and at public events attended by large numbers of young people, brings into question the role of young people in these places. Slogans associated with official institutions, such as 'Medellín: a home for life' and 'Antioquia: the most educated region', contrast starkly with their impoverished political and social reality.

In Medellín CONVIVIR ('Special vigilance and private security services' – a network of anti-guerilla neighbourhood watch groups) and paramilitary groups - offer, by means of extortion, private security services - mainly in areas where there are businesses, massage parlours, night clubs, bars and other places where sexual exploitation and drug dealing occur. Indeed, many of these places are under the management of these paramilitary groups.[11]

Furthermore, an issue that has been neglected by the state and the justice system (apart from sporadic references in declarations of the law of justice and peace), and which has been ignored by the media, is sexual violence against women as a weapon of war.[12] Although since sexism and chauvinism can of course exist under an oppressive system such as patriarchy independently of war, rape and physical abuse against women and girls during the armed conflict have been a systematic and premeditated way of exercising control and fear in communities.[13] These assaults have mainly been carried out by paramilitaries.[14]

The high rate of femicide in Antioquia, substantiates this conclusion. In 2011, 270 women were murdered in Antioquia (119 of them in Medellín). Research is needed as to whether these figures correlate with the return of men from disbanded paramilitaries.

Conclusion

Colombia is a country which is impoverished, militarised and highly influenced by right-wing ideals. More than 15.2 million people are living in poverty, 4.7 million of them in abject poverty.[15] The structural and cultural causes of the armed social conflict are ignored. Military institutions interfere intensely in communities' social lives, and this affects young people the most: in addition to the large number of forced recruitments, the Civic Youth Police (made up of boys and girls of seven to eighteen years of age) is growing in the country's main cities, where paramilitary organisations control large areas.

Notes

1   'Para-state' refers to entities that purport to exercise state-like authority in a particular territory.
2   Ricardo Arias, 'Los sucesos del 9 de abril de 1948 como legitimadores de la violencia oficial', Biblioteca Luis Ángel Arango del Banco de la República. <www.banrepcultural.org/blaavirtual/revistas/rhcritica/arias.htm> (accessed September 2012).
3   Ariel Sánchez Meertens and Gonzalo Sánchez, 'Mayo 27 de 1964: El huevo de la serpiente', Semana, 2008. <www.semana.com/wf_ImprimirArticulo.aspx?IdArt=78976> (accessed September 2012).
4   Eduardo Pizarro Leongómez, 'Marquetalia: el mito fundacional de las FARC', UNP, 57 (2004). [Online at http://historico.unperiodico.unal.edu.co/Ediciones/57/03.htm (accessed October 2012).
5   Daniel Cristancho, 'Entre pájaros y chulavitas: Relato de la tradición oral campesina sobre el conflicto político, social y armado de Colombia', Agencia Prensa Rural, 2011. <http://prensarural.org/spip/spip.php?article5176> (accessed September 2012).
6   Camilo García, 'Lo sagrado y la violencia. Raíces de la violencia actual en Colombia', Revista Numero. <www.revistanumero.com/38sagra.htm> (accessed October 2012).
7   Asamblea Permanente de la Sociedad Civil por la Paz, 'Costos y efectos de la guerra en Colombia', 2011. <http://alfresco.uclouvain.be/alfresco/d/d/workspace/SpacesStore/c54ac c30-cada-4290-ae1f-252f9910983d/Costos%20y%20efectos%20de%20la%20guerra%20 en%20Colombia-%20Velandia%202011.pdf> (accessed September 2012), p. 14.
8   Ibid, p. 16. Both figures rounded to the nearest billion.

9 Ibid, p. 25.
10 VerdadAbierta.com, 'Paramilitarismo y conflicto armado en Colombia. Paramilitares continúan atacando a defensores de Derechos Humanos', 2011. <http://verdadabierta.com/bandera/index.php?option=com_content&id=3901> (accessed September 2012).
11 Elmundo.com, 'Convivir, la seguridad en manos de los ilegales', 2012. <www.elmundo.com/portal/movil.detalle.php?idx=178431> (accessed September 2012).
12 VerdadAbierta.com, 'Paramilitarismo y conflicto armado en Colombia. Batallas de hombres en cuerpos de mujeres', 2009. <www.verdadabierta.com/nunca-mas/41-violencia-contra-mujeres/801-batallas-de-hombres-en-cuerpos-de-mujeres> (accessed September 2012).
13 Ibid.
14 Lapluma.net, 'IV Semana por la Memoria: Mujeres y Guerra. Víctimas y resistentes en el Caribe colombiano', 2011. <www.es.lapluma.net/index.php?option=com_content&view=a rticle&id=2914:iv-semana-por-la-memoria-mujeres-y-guerra-victimas-y-resistentes-en-el-caribe-colombiano&catid=90:impunidad&Itemid=422> (accessed 31 May 2013).
15 Elespectador.com, 'Pobreza en Colombia afectó al 34,1% de la población en 2011', 2012. <www.elespectador.com/economia/articulo-346885-pobreza-colombia-afecto-al-341-de-poblacion-2011> (accessed September 2012).

Translated from the original Spanish by Rebecca House

Shaping the Debate: Militarising Public Discourse and Education

Survey findings: Public discourse

In many countries (twenty of the thirty-two), celebrities are used to promote the military. By contrast in Kenya, the military is almost secretive (although the Maroon Commandos, a band, are very popular).

The military in half of the countries have a website aimed specifically at young people. Although Switzerland doesn't, its military does sponsor youth websites. Approximately two-thirds use either Facebook or YouTube, and others have an 'unofficial' presence (content uploaded by current or ex-military personnel or others). Ten militaries produce a magazine targeted at young people. Potentially, this number will decrease as reliance on the internet increases. Similarly, eight countries have a military radio station; others have a television channel or dedicated programme. Twenty-two countries have memorial days for military personnel – Finland's is unusually named after a specific person.

A majority – twenty-five of the thirty-two countries – heroise injured and dead military personnel, at least on a rhetorical level, and in the public discourse of twenty-three countries, military personnel in general are heroised. In some cases – like Finland and Kenya – this primarily applies to historical figures, whilst elsewhere it is a general trend.

In eleven of countries surveyed, the idea that being in the military gives meaning to your life is prominent. In Austria, this is extended to mean that military service is seen as 'a necessity for learning social behaviour'. In Kenya, however, the military is perceived primarily as a source of employment, in a context where unemployment is high.

More rare in the survey results was the idea that the military's engagement in combat is only and always for 'defence' (including the defence of a society's values) - only in Turkish-administered Northern Cyprus, Turkey, Argentina and Paraguay.

The military is regarded as apolitical in just six countries. In some countries where the military is seen as political, this is very explicit - for example in Mozambique the President is also commander-in-chief of Armed Forces, and his brother is Defence Minister, and in Turkish-administered Northern Cyprus where the military is directly involved in party politics. In Finland, the military is seen as representing the whole of the political spectrum, and this is actually used as an argument for conscription: a defence against coups.

Again in all but six countries, there is the general belief that there are malevolent people or countries in the world from whom the public must be defended by military force. In twenty-one of these countries, the enemy is a specific person or country. Some of these threats are common to several countries – such as 'Terrorists' and 'Al Queda' – whilst others are very specific to the country in question (for example Pakistan for India, Bolivia in Paraguay, Al Shabab - Somalian militant Islamists – in Kenya). In Macedonia, who or what the threat is depends on your ethnicity.

In a different twenty-one countries there is a sense of fear among the general public about these threats. In twenty-two countries, there seems to have been a return of or increase in patriotic values over the last decade, though with some important intra-country regional variations, for example there has been this increase in the Basque Country, but not in the rest of the state of Spain.

Quotes from WRI's Countering the Militarisation of Youth conference

> They are constantly selling the idea that Venezuela is going to be invaded by the United States and in the face of this external threat...there is a permanent feeling of being on the verge of war or armed conflict...They always say that the United State wants Venezuela's oil, however our president Chávez negotiated with transnational energy companies for 30 to 40 years. This means that that argument is invalid... - Rafael Uzcategui, Venezuela

> World War I especially is toted as being the catalysing factor of Canada as a nation. Because up until then we had been simply a British colony. This argument that World War I and our participation in warfare – and our distinguishing ourselves in warfare – is what actually moved us to be sort of a sovereign, or a separate, entity. So there is a glorification of the soldier and of battle that is brought out... - Christel LeBlanc, Canada

> They do advertise of course, because they have to persuade people "The army's there to protect you – the army's there to build the peace"...The media praise them a lot, and try really hard to make

them look nice: "They protect us. And if they weren't there on the border between North Korea and South Korea, who knows what would to happen to us." You wouldn't even recognise soldier-related things in the media 'cause it's so usual, and that's why it's more dangerous...TV stars and movie stars, if they're male and if they are up to the age that they have to join the military, are really praised if they choose to go, especially if they choose the navy or the air force instead [a longer service], and any who doesn't do military service is gonna be damned - their career's over. So I think that influences the young generation a lot, 'cause they're like the heroes to them right? - Garam Jang, South Korea

Some television series and shows are partly funded by the Ministry of Defence provided that the army can present itself positively in them. Solely positive aspects – for example adventure - are shown, so that people develop an interest... - Geart Bosma, Netherlands

One of the arguments that they bring up is that you need to serve the country to protect your own people against possible threats – threats which are not even identified. It's the hero element, in which you need to be a hero to protect your sisters, your brothers and everything. And another argument is that of discipline – to say they want to discipline young people because they feel they're involved in so many socially-negative elements within the community of South Africa. - Kaizer Tshehla, South Africa

Because there is mandatory conscription, there's this feeling that everybody goes to the army – everyone has to do their part in society, and the moment that you don't, you're treated as a parasite, using the protection of the army just by living in the country, but not doing your part. The two biggest radio stations in Israel are owned and run by the army – that's what everyone hears. And every single news article that has to do with the army has to have a response of the army spokesperson, so if the army spokesperson is now not talking to you because he didn't like the last report that you wrote, you can't issue another. - Sahar Vardi, Israel

They're also normalising the military and war, in the way that they talk about working at the military as a regular job... - Cattis Laska, Sweden

I'm not saying people shouldn't feel pride or shouldn't feel whatever they feel. But there's not much critical thinking going into

Survey findings - Education

In eighteen of the countries surveyed there is an official collaboration between the military and the Ministry of Education. In eleven countries - all in Europe, the Middle East and North America - schools have to allow visits by military personnel. In nine countries schools are visited by military veterans. Armed forces (or other militaristic agencies) in the same number of countries – including six where there is no obligation to allow a military presence in schools - provide training for teachers. In Macedonia, Serbia, Republic of Ireland, Kenya, Mozambique, and Tunisia the military is not present in the education system.

In fourteen countries the main purpose of military presence in the education system is to promote uncritical support of the military; in eleven it is recruitment. Less common reasons for their involvement are the commemoration of military history (Canada), promoting military schools (Greece) and providing cheap teachers (Israel). In Belgium, France, Germany, Greece, Russia, Sweden, UK, USA, and South Africa the military does overt recruitment in schools; in many other countries their recruitment activities are more subtle.

In most cases where the armed forces are present in schools, they give lessons to the students (most notably History and Social Sciences). In the UK and in Israel the military also help individual pupils with their studies. In six countries they also provide lesson plans. In sixteen countries, the civil curriculum also includes textbooks and other resources with militaristic symbols, or which promote militarism in other ways - especially in History.

In Russia, Ecuador and Israel there is compulsory pre-military training as part of the school curriculum, either at schools or military bases (in other countries this only occurs in military academies/colleges). In those countries where schools do not pass students' details onto the military systematically, there are other ways that this may occur. For example, in Switzerland, students have a day off school to attend an army information day.

The militarisation of education also exists outside of schools. In eight countries the armed forces have youth groups or movements; in Russia and Israel there are highly militarised non-military youth groups. In fifteen countries the military provides camps or summer camps for students, and in eight countries schools take students to these camps.

General perceptions of whether the military's involvement in education is a positive thing, vary a lot. In Belgium, Finland, France, Canada, and India, it is not seen as a positive thing, but it is not seen as a negative thing either: most people just don't recognise the military as having much of a role. In the UK and Paraguay, many people appreciate the idea that the military can instil discipline among students.

Quotes from WRI's Countering the Militarisation of Youth conference

In our school we had a Reserve Officer Training Corps programme, which they say is not necessarily for recruitment – it's for leadership, development and discipline but you get to play soldier. - Kelly Dougherty, USA

The Cadets [for 14-18 year-olds] is one of the other things that entices the youth to join the military, because they see the pride in them and their uniform. As a military man people show respect – people are afraid of you: "Hey, the military man is coming". You have militia men who come and train them one or two days, how to handle the gun, and then the marching, and self-discipline. So by the time the students are at university, they have already developed an interest in joining the army. And at university we even went to the jungle. A week, with this kind of training – you develop so much interest that you wish to be part of the military. - Samuel Koduh, Ghana

It's usually a pair of soldiers who come to the jobs fair for graduating students. They'll be sitting at a desk, maybe with a display of the different sorts of jobs – interesting, fun, meaningful jobs - that you can have in the military. - Christel LeBlanc, Canada

Some teachers take the children to a military show, or to the show of the special police forces, where there are lots of weapons and...vehicles and stuff. And kids play and take pictures with guns and stuff. - Boro Kitanoski, Macedonia

I give lessons on peace in schools. When I speak to the teachers I often notice that they have a military definition of "peace" – namely that military missions are necessary for acquiring it. - Geart Bosma, Netherlands

In kindergarten you bring gifts to soldiers. And then later there's worksheets to teach children how to count: you have on one hand the numbers 1 to 10, and on the other different numbers of symbols like tanks and aeroplanes. You have to join them up. The most you see the military is in high school: you have soldiers from the Educational Corps coming in explaining to the children the different positions in the army, and teaching, and in the eleventh grade there is a week where the whole class goes to a military base and goes through kind of basic training – shooting...things of the sort. - Sahar Vardi, Israel

'Die for your country': Turning to bravery, loyalty and honour in order to legitimise war and recruit soldiers in Germany

Jonna Schürkes

Persuading the German people that German soldiers - many of them young - should go to war is not an easy endeavour. Every militarist tries to do so and each one has a different explanation for people's reluctance. The president of Germany, Joachim Gauck, sees it as denial by those who prefer not to acknowledge the fact that German soldiers are still getting killed and injured in combat. He laments how people are not ready to sacrifice themselves for society because of their egoism, saying "'[these people] all too easily forget that a functional democracy also requires effort, attention, bravery and sometimes even the utmost that a man can offer: his life, his own life!'" He also complains about people who come to the wrong conclusions through their knowledge of German history: "'...'Count us out' as a pure reflex is not an appropriate stance if we are to take our past seriously'".[1]

Making Germany's past war crimes into an obligation to engage in military intervention in other countries, to prepare (often young) people for killing others and coming back from war physically and psychologically damaged (or not at all), is an enormous feat which the German politician Joseph Fischer emphasised by declaring: "I've not only learnt: never again war! But I've also learnt: never again Auschwitz".[2] In this way he justified the participation of the German Armed Forces in the war between NATO and Yugoslavia.

However, several surveys indicate that the German public's reluctance for foreign missions is on the rise, despite all attempts made to enlist peoples' support through reasoning. Yet the usual reasons given by interviewees are ambiguous: are they refusing this commitment because they think that the people in the countries where German forces intervene suffer, rather than benefit, from the soldiers' presence; or are they rather of the opinion that this form of help is simply not financially viable in the face of the economic crisis and the increasing number of German soldiers killed in combat?

Since militarists now seem to increasingly assert the latter argument, military interventions are now clearly being justified by economic interests and geostrategies. While the former president of the Federal Republic was harshly criticised for stating this during his term of office, for which he was obliged to resign, it is obvious that for the Minister of Defence "'our interests and our place in the world are fundamentally determined by our role as an exporting nation and high-tech country in Central Europe. Consequently, we have a national interest to have access by land, sea and air.'"[3] This may help to convince people who are afraid that the price of war could be higher than its economic benefits. But the death of German soldiers can't be justified in this way. It's necessary to appeal to people with values such as patriotism, pride, homeland, bravery, readiness to make sacrifices, and overcoming self-centred wishful thinking.

In April 2010 the mandate for the intervention of the Federal Armed Forces was to be renewed. The loss of three German soldiers was used by Angela Merkel not only to promote the prolonging of the intervention but also to influence public opinion. She said that the fallen soldiers were courageous "'because they accomplished their duty of defending our rights and our freedom, fully aware that they were risking life and limb'", loyally serving their country. Merkel cited Helmut Schmidt, who in 2008 swore on oath that German soldiers were not being abused by the state: "'Yes...this State...asks a lot of its soldiers, a lot indeed, as has recently become painfully clear. However it will never abuse them. It puts them at the service of free and democratic values of this nation.'" Moreover, she repeated the oath sworn by every recruit: "'I swear to serve loyally the Federal Republic of Germany and to defend courageously the rights and the freedom of German people.'" She demonstrated the soldiers` courage by telling the story of one who was awarded a medal of honour for saving a group of his comrades from an ambush by shooting an Afghan soldier. Before explaining why she believed the interventions by the Federal Armed Forces were necessary, she also alluded to Obama's words: "'The soldier's courage and sacrifice is full of glory, expressing devotion to country, to cause, to comrades in arms.'"[4]

Soldiers receiving the Cross for Honour from Defence Minister Thomas de Maizière in November 2011 (credit - Bundeswehr-Fotos Wir.Dienen.Deutschland.)

Representing people's deaths as a service to the nation, and what they do as courageous and brave, not only expresses the aim of renewing the intervention mandate in order to participate in the war in Afghanistan, but it also helps the attempts to keep soldiers (and their sphere) in line and to convince young people to join the armed forces to participate in this war and future wars. Thus the military's current campaign (which started in 2011) to increase recruitment concentrates on concepts such as bravery, loyalty, honour and homeland: 'We serve Germany' affirms the motto.

The posters which, with this slogan, advertise military service, demonstrate what lies behind each individual word: 'we' as 'comradeship' - where women are looking up to strong men; 'serve' as in sacrificing one's own life, and 'Germany' as homeland, which is represented by people painted in black, red and yellow, by the waving of German flags, and through the pictures of families and senior citizens being entertained on a military boat, with 'Germany is rich and respected' written above them.[5]

The lack of appeal these values have to young people is lamented in the most recent report by the youth officers (Jugendoffiziere), who are responsible for advertising war as necessary and military service as honourable. It is said that young people are little inclined to make a 'personal contribution' to establish 'peace through freedom'.

Of course only their concept of peace and freedom is considered valid, and the 'personal contribution' entails going to war. The report claims that 'by exchanging views with young people the youth officers establish that the clearly individual perspectives of role models within families or circles of friends are somewhat taken on without critical reflection. The tenor is at times stereotypically, polemically, and even partly radically, shaped. In such cases the teachers are acting pedagogically by involving the youth officers.'[6]

A potent mixture is concocted for this concept: war as the way of carrying out economic interests, participation in these wars as a service to society, death as sacrifice for the homeland, killing as bravery.

Notes

1 Joachim Gauck, first official Armed Firces visit, Hamburg, 12 June 2012. <www.bundespraesident.de/SharedDocs/Reden/DE/Joachim-Gauck/Reden/2012/06/120612-Bundeswehr.html> (accessed December 2012).
2 Joschka Fischer, 'Ich habe gelernt: Nie wieder Auschwitz', *Süddeutsche Zeitung*, 24 January 2005. <http://www.sueddeutsche.de/politik/fischer-ich-habe-gelernt-nie-wieder-auschwitz-1.915701> (accessed December 2012).
3 Thomas de Maizière, Reorientation of the Bundeswehr speech, Berlin, 18 May 2011.
4 Minutes from Darmstadt conference plenary 17/37, 22 April 2010.

5 Bundeswehr, 'Wir. Dienen. Deutschland.' <www.wirdienendeutschland.de> (accessed June 2012).
6 Annual report of the youth officers, 2011. (accessed 23 May 2012).

Translated from the original German by Eleonora Romagna and Richard Meakin

Young people in Turkey besieged by militarism: Past and present

Militarism has a long history in Turkey. It is therefore surprising that there are very few studies in the Social Sciences and in Education on how the militarisation of young people has operated. With a few exceptions, social scientists have remained silent when it comes to questioning the military and the way militarism has been instilled in young people, one generation after another.

Militarism after the Ottoman Empire

The Ottoman Empire lasted for centuries and always relied on its military might, but militarism was not a part of everyday life. Militarism was only introduced into daily life with the advent of modern institutions, particularly schools, which became part of the state apparatus when the Ottoman Empire was succeeded by a new nation state - the Republic of Turkey - in 1923. The founders of the republic were determined to break with the past and modernise the country. There was, however, an inherent contradiction in that their modernist vision was limited by their military roots. The leading reformers were all military men and, in keeping with the military tradition, all believed in the authority and the sacredness of the state. The public also believed in the military. It was the military, after all, who led the the War of Liberation (1919-1923) and saved the motherland.

The founders of the new state believed in education: the new republic could only be built through an educational campaign. Recurrent wars of the late Ottoman period and the War of Liberation itself produced a large number of orphaned, sick or frail children, who needed the protection and education that the state could offer. The authoritarian regime assumed that discipline was essential to creating a modern citizenry (well-educated, healthy and dutiful men and women) from the largely uneducated masses, and that quick but orderly social progress could be achieved through regulating many spheres of life.

Two primary goals, establishing national unity and modernising the country, were often conceived in a militaristic framework: the transformation of the human body in line with modern, rational and scientific values in many spheres of life - including clothing, aesthetics, health, reproduction, childcare and housekeeping. Disciplining the public through body politics was essential to creating modern citizens. These notions evolved in the 1930s into eugenics. Eugenics was popular in the modern world and the republican leaders imported eugenics to support the state's regulation of the human body: abortion was abolished, pre-marital examination of couples was mandated, childcare institutions were established. Prevention of epidemics and alcoholism became a priority. Under the nation-building frenzy, a collectivist and authoritarian discourse emerged, producing an ultra-nationalist ideology that bordered on racism. Militarism thrived in this climate.

Militarism after 1945

A new world order was established after World War II. In Turkey a liberal government that aligned itself with conservative social forces ended the single-party regime. The new government was not against militaristic practices in schools, except those that did not fit with gender segregation. The new government pushed some of the reforms back but the military coup in 1960 put an end to this.

The military coup introduced yet another contradiction. It paved the way to a progressive constitution. But it also legitimised the role of military forces as protectors of the state. Using this role, the military would intervene in 1971 and 1980. The military always did its best to gain public support before and after each intervention.

With the 1960 constitution a vibrant political climate emerged. However, two parties dominated politics until 1980: a left-of-centre party that represented the heavy-handed and authoritarian republican tradition, and a right-of-centre party that aligned with conservative forces – including religious movements – in the service of capitalism. Both parties regarded schools as the breeding ground of social forces, and schools became the battleground between so-called 'progressive' and 'reactionary' forces.

The regime change and the political debates that followed did not influence militarism in schools. By 1945, militarism was part-and-parcel of school life and the progressive 1960 constitution did not challenge that. It was military intervention, after all, that had made a new constitution possible, and many regarded the military as a progressive social force.

The coup

In 1980, the political regime was transformed. First, a set of 'liberal reforms' was introduced. Next, a military coup imposed a reign of ruthless terror. The military eliminated all political movements and democratic institutions. As the military cleared the path to a neoliberal economy, it solidified ideological control over all scientific, cultural and educational affairs. In 1982 a new constitution established an authoritarian framework, which increased the power of executive bodies. In 1983, Turgut Özal, chief architect of these reforms, came to power, serving as prime minister for two consecutive terms and later as president (1989-1993).

The new authoritarian regime promoted 'Turkish-Islamic Synthesis', a conservative doctrine that was produced to offset socialist influences. The official ideology had always promoted nationalism and militarism. Ultra-nationalists propagated the idea that Turks were a 'military nation'. But nationalism was not sufficient to deter socialism. Religion would be a much stronger antidote. In line with this doctrine, the 1982 constitution mandated religious education in schools.

Teacher training institutions were always seen as a key way of producing the ideal teacher. In the 1970s, these institutions became a major battleground between 'progressive' and 'reactionary' forces and were controlled by ultra-nationalists by the end of the decade. After the coup, these institutions were officially cleansed of the leftist elements. Soon these institutions were producing large numbers of teachers who were equipped with the Turkish-Islamic Synthesis. By 1984, these new teachers were in classrooms. The military government introduced strict dress codes for teachers and students, and got rid of leftist teachers. Özal's MPs endorsed these policies; schools turned into more dogmatic and militaristic institutions.

Militarism in schools

Schools around the world provide fertile ground for militarism: there is a captive audience, a comprehensive mandate, a hierarchical structure and a clear power differential between students and professionals. Schools can easily be turned into paramilitary institutions.

Militarism is often not transmitted or sustained by direct contact with the military. Rather, schools and other civilian institutions help military approaches to permeate daily practices and belief systems. Unlike mandatory military service, schools are very systematic and persistent: mandatory schooling reaches almost all children, and does so over many years. Children as young as 5 or 6 can encounter militarism at school.

School as a boot camp

A typical school has elements of militarism such as domination, submission, discipline and violence embedded in it. Violence towards students produces violence among students, and student violence is used to justify institutional violence in the form of militarism.

A typical school provides a wide variety of militaristic experiences, some more obvious than others. School life is supposed to be 'orderly' and 'disciplined': students are expected to follow military-style rules and routines and expect punishment if they do not.

Inside the school, flags and symbols of nationalism are everywhere. Kings and their conquests are glorified on the walls. Commemorations are common and they are either about military victories or performed in military style. A typical school has very little to remind students of peace, nonviolence and youthfulness.

Physical education is where military order - such as forming ranks and marching in unison – is taught. From early on, students learn to stand to attention immediately when they are told to. A typical student has to do this countless times in both elementary and high school.

Students are just like foot soldiers. They can be 'at ease' only when adults are not around. They are expected to be respectful, and respect begins with submission. Students stand up when a teacher walks in. The curriculum emphasises duties and obligations much more than rights and freedoms. Overall the curriculum is now less nationalistic, but these military-like practices endure on a daily basis.

Ceremonies and uniforms

Ceremonies – such as those in schools - are important for militarism; they help it to grow. The school week in Turkey opens and ends with a ceremony. In the opening ceremony the flag is raised and the national anthem is sung. In nationalist eyes, this is a sacred ritual. Everybody has to stand to attention. Students often get scolded, humiliated or disciplined for not being 'solemn' enough during the ceremony. In elementary schools each day begins with an archaic nationalist pledge.

Students are also expected to participate in certain official ceremonies outside of the school. On various occasions students are asked to wear a military uniform and hold a weapon. During Police Week it is common to see children in police uniforms. On Children's Day (23 April) until recently a very militaristic official event was held in each city in a sports stadium.

Conflict and martyrdom

Militarism needs conflict. Open conflict is best because it justifies the war machine. If martyrdom is embraced by tradition and propagated in schools, casualties can also fuel militarism.

The Republic of Turkey was founded after the War of Liberation and martyrdom has been an element of the nationalist ideology ever since. With time, martyrdom has become a legitimising tool for the Armed Forces. Now, martyrdom is a versatile tool for politicians who want to to justify violence and its natural outcome, death.

The state has been fighting with the Kurdistan Workers' Party (PKK) since 1984.[1] While dead bodies piled up and millions of civilians suffered human rights abuses, martyrdom was used to glorify death, thereby legitimising the ongoing violence. Massive public relations campaigns were launched to fuel militarism, including the coordinated effort to commemorate the Battle of Gallipoli, which in Turkey is often called the Çanakkale Victory. This was not an ordinary battle. It was a war of attrition in which thousands of soldiers on both sides had to endure extreme conditions for months. Many died needlessly - not in combat but of hunger, disease or from falling into open latrines and drowning. But the commemorations framed it as a victory achieved through martyrdom.

Militaristic school ceremonies were organised on the day associated with the victory (18 March 1915).[2] Many schools organized trips to Gelibolu (Gallipoli) to commemorate the victory and pay homage to the martyrs. Soon this was transformed into a continuous pilgrimage. Huge numbers of students and adults were taken there. The message was clear: 'We are a strong nation and even the mightiest power cannot conquer us. We are all ready to fight and to die, if necessary.'

The effort to polarise public opinion was nasty. During a demonstration in Mersin in March 2005, two youths were handed a flag, which they soon destroyed. This was portrayed in the media as a desecration of the Turkish flag by Kurds. It turned out to be a setup, but not until after it had had its desired effect: flags started appearing everywhere, including schools. Schools were infused with even more signs of nationalism and militarism. About two years later, another school commemoration was instituted: 12 March - the day in 1921 when the national anthem was adopted.

Private schools

Private schools in Turkey are often portrayed as model schools. Private schools used to serve the children of the elite and therefore it was assumed that they were less militaristic. This is not true. Many private schools organise pilgramages to Gelibolu. A very expensive private school in Bodrum, for instance, held an event where pre-school students were dressed in military uniforms or flag dresses.[3]

A trip organised by a private school in Kayseri illustrates the problem. Students in uniforms were taken to nearby Mount Erciyes, where they re-enacted a battle under snowfall. Local authories and media were present. Also invited were the director and the leading actor of a film glorifying 'child martyrs'.[4] The head of the Provincial Education Directorate was very happy. The ceremony, he said, taught children 'love for the homeland, the flag and the country'.

What's in a name?

Militarism thrives on hatred. Public areas can be used to mark a conflict and instil in daily life elements that remind everyone of conflict and hatred. As institutions central to public life, schools can be used as markers of conflict and

A poster distributed to the media by the Army General Staff Headquarters in 2010, just before Martyrs' Day (18 March). The slogan reads: 'My Martyr! What you entrusted me with is my honour.' (credit - Serdar M. Değirmencioğlu)

serve the function of perpetuating hatred and violence.

That is exactly what has happened in Turkey. Many schools across the country are now named after a military martyr, transforming them into public tombstones. Some other public areas (such as parks) and institutions (such as health centers) have also been targets of this sort of militarism.

Militarism is still strong

For more than ten years the Justice and Development Party (JDP) has been in power. The JDP appears determined to dismantle old institutions, including the constitution put in place by the military government in 1982, and has earned a reputation as a pro-democracy party despite the fact that it is clearly the product of the political climate that the military regime created.[5]

Because the military has always defined itself as a secular power and a protector of secularism, and forced a coalition government led by a predecessor of the JDP to resign in 1997, the JDP has seen the military as an obstacle and curbed its power drastically. For many, the JDP's reforms and election victories are democracy in action. To more crticial observers, however, the JDP agenda reflects authoritarian and oppressive policies that serve a neoliberal and a neo-conservative order. As the JDP's hold on power has been consolidated, the regime has become more and more like single-party rule. Party leaders allow little criticism or debate, even within their own ranks.

The apparent reformist character of the the JDP stems from the determination of its leaders to break away with the heavy-handed Republican tradition. It relies less on the state apparatus and more on local government, local conservative NGOs, and an obedient media. Until recently the army was used as the ultimate force whenever needed. The new order regards the police as safer to deploy because the police is directly controlled by the government. The ultimate force that sustains the neo-conservative order is, of course, religion.[6]

Many observers fail to understand the fact that militarism in Turkey is alive and well. The military has lost its power but efforts to glorify martyrdom and to pump up nationalism and religion still continue. Over recent years increasingly bigger commemorations have been held in schools for the martyrs of the Battle of Sarıkamış (December 1914 - January 1915). In January 2013, the Ministry of Youth and Sports organised the largest commemoration in history, accompanied by a number of religious ceremonies.

One of the most popular policies of the JDP has been the creation of the Housing Development Administration (HDA), which is overseen by the Prime Minister's Office and is in charge of all major construction projects across the country. The HDA has built many new residential areas, each with a mosque and often with a school; many of these schools are named after a military 'martyr' who was killed in the war against the PKK.

The leader of the JDP himself is not shy about employing militarism. He has used martyrdom regularly in his speeches and boasts of his party's intentions to produce 'faithful and vindictive' generations.[7] The JDP is eager to leave old-style nationalist militarism behind and replace it with a militarism guided by militant Islam.

Militarism is also very visible in local government. Across Turkey, most municipalities are controlled by the JDP. Its mayors are consolidating an authoritarian conservative order in their area. Sincan, for instance, is a big municipality in metropolitan Ankara and is the bastion of JDP, boasting more than twenty parks all named after 'martyrs'.

These developments are very worrying. As militant Islam replaces militant nationalism as the overarching ideology, militarism is becoming ever more dangerous. Nationalism is a human product. Islam, on the other hand, is portrayed as God-given and therefore cannot be challenged. Religion can provide militarism a very effective shield and access to various domains that militarism was not previously able to penetrate. This mix of militarism and religion is harder to resist and to defeat. As the state in Turkey becomes less secular, young people in particular are being subjected to an increasingly more militaristic and totalitarian order.

Notes

1   As this article was being written, a truce came into effect and an agreement was being neared.
2   Videos of these ceremonies are available on YouTube. A very recent example is a private school performance of a play called 'Gözlerim Çanakkale'de Kaldı' (My heart is with you in Çanakkale) [Online at www.youtube.com/watch?v=RpkLH4ZSPpw (accessed 15 May 2013)].
3   Many private schools in Turkey are now associated with religious movements and the degree of militarism in these schools varies according to religious beliefs.
4   The children were martyrs because they supplied ammunition to troops during WWI and froze to death in a blizzard.
5   Over the years the JDP has benefited from a power vacuum and unfair election regulations – both a product of the 1980s. The fact that only fifteen months after it was founded in 2001 the JDP received about a 35 percent vote is a clear indication of the volatile political climate. In only three years, the JDP gained control over municipalities in most major cities, with about 42 percent of the vote. In the 2007 elections the JDP increased its vote to about 47 percent. In 2011 it received almost 50 percent of the vote.
6   The JDP's economic policies produce more wealth, but it is distributed unequally, as reflected in the increase in poverty. This appears to contradict the popular support for the JDP, which has not declined. It seems that it has the tools to achieve popular consent despite the fact that millions live in poor economic conditions.
7   Ekin Karaca, 'Religious Generation versus Liberal Education?', *bianet*, 8 February 2012. <http://bianet.org/english/religion/136000-religious-generation-versus-liberal-education> (accessed 15 May 2013).

Violence, military service, and the education system in Chile

Dan Contreras

In order to relate militarisation and youth in Chile, we must look to the past and recognise the hundreds of years of militarism in the history of this region. Chile has seen territorial and violent occupations by European colonists, the construction of 'homeland heroes' as the core motivational idea behind patriotism, the legalisation of mandatory military training, huge increases in military spending as compared to social spending, the incorporation of military practices within civilian schools, among many other examples. The brunt of these actions has been born by the population's most economically vulnerable group, but potentially the strongest in political terms: the country's boys, girls and young adults. The vulnerability of this segment of the population has allowed it to be exposed to militarisation with ease; potential pockets of resistance are neutralised.

Today, militarism is instilled in society through three different approaches:

1) by perpetrating real violence, exemplified by what is going on in the south of the country against the Mapuche people

2) by legally forcing young people to join the armed forces

3) by creating myths through the formal education system.

These three approaches, some of which are medium or long term, complement each other but also stand alone, depending on the particular objectives of the state and it armed forces.

Territorial militarisation and disproportionate violence on Mapuche territory

While this article was being written, the Santiago headquarters of the UN agency UNICEF were occupied by Mapuche women and mothers in protest against police attacks on little children during raids and interventions on indigenous territory. Thanks to mass access to information, we were able to see the bodies of boys and girls bleeding as a result of pellets fired by the security forces. Sadly, this information is not immediately transmitted via mainstream television stations, newspapers or legal radio broadcasts, but rather by the alternative - and often self-managed - media that logically reacts against prohibitive and authoritarian policies that encourage violence and militarisation.

While the Chilean state's harassment of the Mapuche people dates back to the nineteenth century, throughout history the state has kept the spirit of conquest alive in different ways: seizing land, engaging in open warfare, and - since the end of the 1990s - raiding communities. The common thread linking all of these colonising practices has been territorial militarisation and disproportionate violence towards the Mapuche people, justified by some event or incident which the state interprets as an act of terrorism. The number of weapons and police forces deployed in southern Chile reveal what appears to be a turf war. However, we must understand that this situation was created unilaterally by the Chilean state through its refusal to acknowledge territorial claims, its failure to help protect and transmit Mapuche culture for the preservation of their ancestral identity, and the forcible removal of the Mapuche people from their land, and denial of their access to it.

All of these actions carried out by the state share the same omnipotent origin; economic power moulded according to the prevailing model. By turning the earth solely into a means of production, the imaginary elements necessary for the survival of any kind of culture and historical memory disappear. This is the constant conflict between the Mapuche people and the Chilean state: on the one hand, a people that refuses to forget its ancestors and its culture, and on the other, a state that strives to generate financial profit for the already wealthy. The two sides speak different languages, and thus the fact that they don't comprehend each other is unsurprising. As long as they remain unequal, agreement cannot be reached. The only side capable of facilitating the conditions for dialogue is the state, by transferring its economic interests to another sector or by serving them in another way. Contrary to this hypothesis, the conflict is worsening: the state is selling off Mapuche territories to big natural resource extraction companies, and is intensifying levels of violence via the police forces.

These actions have had a negative effect not only on the Mapuche people, but also on all who live in the region. It is significant that the Aruacania region, the area we are talking about, is the poorest region in Chile, where 23% of the population lives in poverty.[1] The paradox lies in the fact that the arrival of the big forestry companies to the region was supposed to bring with it big employment opportunities, especially for people without qualifications or training. What happened? The extraction industries use modern machinery that can be operated by a minimal number of people, thus reducing employment opportunities. The state's justifications for the use and administration of the territories are similar to the arguments of someone selling a product: that it works, that it will be beneficial for everyone, that it will be sustainable. The difference is that, upon request, the buyer can return a product with a request for a refund. In the case of the state, such requests dissipate into thin air, and in return, violence is dealt out.

While the violence has been initiated by the Chilean state, some of the young people's responses have also been violent, which has created a vicious, unfair and brutal cycle for the communities. This in turn has led to violations of human rights, some Mapuche deaths, and the arrest of community leaders, among other things.

At the same time the UNICEF headquarters were being occupied, state and police representatives gathered in the south to hold the so-called 'security summit'. It was here that the ideas of how to confront the groups, mostly comprising violent Mapuche youths, were created. It would seem that in the new strategy, old-time militarisation is still considered to be an adequate response to the conflict. There is no attempt to resolve it through such participatory politics as dialogue and discussion. The future of this region continues to look very similar to the past, entailing the suffering of both the Mapuches and Winkas (meaning Chileans in the Mapudungun language), and the writing of history in blood and fire.

Military service is mandatory

Chile has an enlistment quota, which the armed forces try to fill with voluntary recruits, and then supplements, if necessary, using mandatory draft by lottery. Most conscripts are in the army. At a certain time of year, in public places and in the media, we are inundated with propaganda for mandatory military service. The images used to advertise military service include a group of young people listening to their instructor very attentively, and a group of soldiers parachuting from a helicopter, showing how engrossing and fun it is to wear the uniform. On the radio, you will hear a dialogue between two men, one of whom is able to repair the other's car due to the training he received during his military service. At first glance, these may not seem like very innovative advertising campaigns, but what is obvious is the significant financial investment that has gone into their production and dissemination, as well as the success among their target audience, in appealing to young people of conscription age to do their military service.

Military service in Chile was formalised in the early twentieth century. With this came the creation of a regular body of men who were available should any armed conflict against an external or internal enemy arise - who had basic knowledge of handling weapons and the workings of the military system. There is no doubt whom the state regarded as the internal enemy during the Pinochet takeover in 1973 and at the beginning of the 1980s. The need for a civil body with some kind of military training quantitatively increases the number of people involved in conflict, while decreasing the chances of fatalities among those with more military training or who are higher up the army ranks. Compulsory military service originated at the time when the landowners deliberately sent their peasants to serve in the armed forces. In this way, the landowners gained a disciplined workforce trained in skills, including the use of arms to defend their property.

Nowadays, subjugation is of a different kind. The social conditions inherent in the capitalist system and the neo-liberal model have moulded young people from the lower rungs of society. The lack of employment opportunities and social exclusion resulting from the Chilean educational system have given rise to circumstances that have greatly benefited the armed forces by creating an 'imaginary world' full of opportunity - for example, the ability to finish secondary studies or vocational training and move swiftly on to the world of civilian work. Considering that a significant percentage of young people in Chile do not complete their secondary education and that youth unemployment is high, young people see compulsory military service as a real opportunity for advancement.

What is the reality? First and foremost, military service is intended for young people aged 17 to 18, in other words, those in the middle of their education. Secondary education in Chile is compulsory according to the constitution, therefore, the armed forces are under legal obligation to offer young people lessons at their bases. This is not done as a favour. Vocational training in the armed forces means necessary routine jobs at whichever barrack has to be fit for visits from high-ranking army officials and for day-to-day maintenance, for example gardening and watering the lawns at the base, cutting conscripted soldiers' hair, and cooking for those living on the premises. We could compile a long list proving that training is a way to reduce the budget by avoiding employing people externally to carry out these tasks, relying on the recruited troops to do them. With regard to entry into the world of civilian work, we don't have exact figures or previous cases, but subjective perception and anecdotal information tells us that this promise isn't kept and that the armed forces justifies themselves by suggesting that nowadays a career in the military is easier to follow for those who have done military service (they are prioritised when applying for military school).

Military service in Chile has been characterised by two important elements. The first, compulsory service, dates back a long time. The second, to professionalise the armed forces, appeared in recent decades. It is noteworthy that when the economic and political situation in Chile was standardised to that of other countries, these other countries made military service voluntary, or simply did away with it in pursuit of the new figure of the professional soldier. Since 2000, the armed forces in Chile have focused their efforts on creating this figure. However, the fact that military service is compulsory is totally apposite to professionalism. In other words, the choice the Chilean state has made is to continue to have a uniform and mandatory body instead of a voluntary and specialised force. It has chosen this, principally, in our opinion, because the benefits of having conscription continue to outweigh those of having professional soldiers.

Nowadays, the compulsory nature of military service isn't perceived at first glance since enrolment is automatic. That is to say, the military has the right to register young men, as the legislation allows the personal information of potential recruits to be passed from the Civil Register of National Identification to the armed forces. This has been going on since 2006. There are currently 21,000 young volunteers, of whom 11,000 are serving this year, meaning that the lottery system doesn't need to be implemented.

We don't have the means to contradict these figures, but we can point out that the dates of voluntary enlistment for military service among men in the last two years have been modified to extend the deadlines. The armed forces had to resort to this measure and carried out a second high-profile propaganda campaign so that volunteer quotas were met. Why did this happen? It wasn't down to direct action taken against military service, but rather to the movement of secondary school students who put the Chilean government in a difficult position. The students' reaction against market education provoked their reflection on other actions which infringe upon young peoples' freedom, such as involuntary military service.

The issue of compulsory military service has not been a priority within national debate for some years, but the emergence of youth protests against the infringements of basic rights has meant that the institution of the military is being questioned. We will see how local anti-military and conscientious objectors groups react to the military's new propaganda campaign.

Military indoctrination in schools

In the syllabuses provided by the ministry of education, a specific dichotomy is expressed. On the one hand, the system is designed to reinforce civic education and draw attention to questionable acts of armed forces in history, for example, the Nazi Holocaust, and the dropping of atomic bombs by the USA. On the other hand, it doesn't criticise local militarism. On the contrary, Chilean military heroes are praised and the country's military 'victories' are focused on, encouraging patriotism and xenophobia. It is believed to be probable that all modern states were built through military conflict. The troops are forgotten about and a few individuals are heralded as heroes. This has nothing to do with whether the country is developed or part of the developing world, but rather with the construction of the figure of the state. Therefore the figures who came to power must be maintained in order to continue justifying the state's existence and the existence of its institutions. Thus we can conclude that militarisation goes beyond weapons and barracks for the purpose of national defence: it is also the birthplace of figures who justify other institutions and cultural constructions.

Portraying the military as something natural and unquestionable means that children and young people see military intervention as 'normal', and that the discourse sustaining it is correct. A clear example of this is the discourse surrounding 'terrorism'. Even children associate terrorism with Islamic groups, Al Qaeda and Osama Bin Laden: the concept itself is overlooked.

Acceptance is reinforced by means of ceremonies held on dates of remembrance for the military, schools pausing lessons to commemorate anniversaries, children dressing in military clothing, and art is devoted to honour the date. There is no questioning of the nature of war.

Moreover, in the day-to-day running of schools, practices are employed that originate in the barracks but which were established, quite some time ago, in civilian life. Other practices that become commonplace for children and young people in their time at school are: school 'police' (pseudo-military brigades that keep order at break times), military bands, uniform, protocol very similar to that at military schools such as short hair, polished shoes, and the display of the institution's emblem.

The only resistance to this, as already mentioned, is the protests by secondary school students. The welfare of our youth and, through them, the future of our society, goes beyond legal or constitutional changes. It also calls for a change in the anti-militaristic culture of the formal education system.

The Chilean military knows very well that it has a privileged position, supported by vast sectors of the country. However, in recent years their fear has grown that our youth will drive radical changes in society, leading to new liberal, non-authoritarian and fairer ways to live. Such a scenario would mean stripping the military forces of all virtue, and thus changing some of the social constructs that have existed since the creation of the Chilean state.

Students from a college in Tucapel, central Chile, marching in a military band to mark the bicentenary of Chilean independence in 2010. Similar marches took place in most of Chile (credit - Claudio Jofré Larenas)

Notes

1   United Nations Development Programme, 'Reducción de la Pobreza y la Desigualdad'. <www.pnud.cl/areas/ReduccionPobreza/datos-pobreza-en-Chile.asp> (accessed 11 April 2013).

Translated from the original Spanish by Rebecca House

The military's influence in UK education

Emma Sangster

The armed forces are increasingly being provided with access to young people within the UK education system – mainly at secondary and further education level but also within universities and even primary schools. In addition to armed forces presentations and other visits to schools and colleges which have been going on for many years, there is a new push to make 'military ethos and skills' a part of school life.

To understand what is driving these practices and policies it is important to look at the wider dynamics between the armed forces and civil society. This article looks briefly at recent initiatives and developments that reflect a new and concerted effort to see the military play a larger role in civil society.

National Recognition

In 2008 the Labour government published the Report of Inquiry into the National Recognition of the Armed Forces. The report was concerned with measures to

> increase the recognition that we give to our Armed Forces - including wearing uniforms in public, the idea of a national Armed Forces Day, greater support for homecoming parades, and an expansion of cadet forces, which we know bring benefit to the Armed Forces and young people alike...[involving] local authorities, voluntary bodies, the private sector and, above all, the people up and down the country who devote their time to running cadet units or military charities, or who need another way of expressing their appreciation for what our Armed Forces do for us.[1]

It made forty recommendations for 'increasing visibility', 'improving contact', 'building understanding' and 'encouraging support' for the Armed Forces.

Under the new coalition government, the 2010 Report on the Task Force of the Military Covenant led to the codifying of the 'moral obligation' between the military, the government and the country in the 2011 Armed Forces Covenant. This outlined a proposal for an Armed Forces Community Covenant which 'has its roots in a successful US scheme in which states and towns (incorporating local government and local service providers, the voluntary sector and private companies) voluntarily pledge support for the military community in their area.'[2]

Some of the ways in which these policies affect young people include:

- Armed Forces Day: This was first held in 2009 and takes place on a Saturday in late June 'so that school children and most working adults would be available to attend events'. Local communities around the country organise parades or an event to celebrate and show support for the Armed Forces. The Armed Forces in turn provide teaching resources for the event. The army's resource for use with children aged 7 to 11, has a section on Real Life Heroes which asks the children to look at a website to find out about different roles within the military 'to see how the qualities you identified for being a hero apply to working for the Armed Forces in keeping our nation safe'.

- Cadets: The government chose Armed Forces Day 2012 to announce funding of nearly £11 million to increase the number of Combined Cadet Forces in state schools. Research into strengthening non-school based cadet units has also been undertaken.

- In schools: The National Inquiry report recommended that an 'understanding' of the armed forces be promoted in schools via the national curriculum, presentations by local Armed Forces units and visits by individual serving men and women to their old schools. Although the Armed Forces already visit thousands of schools each year, these recommendations, and the recent Department for Education 'military ethos and skills' policy, indicates that this is increasingly being led by central government and is not a matter for individual schools to determine.

- Community Covenants: By late 2012 half the local authorities in the UK had signed a covenant 'to encourage local communities to support the service community in their area and promote understanding and awareness among the public of issues affecting the armed forces community.' So far, £5 million worth of central government funding has been used to promote the scheme and for grants to local initiatives including those that involve children and young people in schools, through play activities.

Future Reserves

In 2012 the Ministry of Defence published a consultation on its strategy for increasing the role of the reserve forces as the number of regular forces is reduced. Future Reserves 2020: Delivering the Nation's Security Together outlines how the

> Reserve Forces will grow (to a trained strength of 30,000 in the Army Reserve) and will be an integral and integrated element of our Armed Forces. While the overall numbers we require are well within historic norms, we will need greater assurance that the reserves will be available for training and deployment when needed.[3]

The intention is that, in order to create a larger pool of potential reserves, a new relationship with communities, employers, reservists and their families will have to be formed. A greater commitment from society will be sought so that a larger number of people who are not professional soldiers are attracted to joining the reserves. Pathways through education and employment will be developed and new roles for reservists, including a new deal in terms of pay, support and recognition, will be on offer.

A new role for the military in public life – an example

When the corporate giant G4 failed to provide adequate security for the 2012 Olympics in London the Armed Forces were seen to save the day when thousands of soldiers stepped in to do the job. At a time when the Armed Forces is seeking to develop a new relationship with civil society, whilst undergoing major restructuring, this was a significant moment. Post-Olympic speculation suggested that politicians may take the success of the Armed Forces in this role as a sign that the public is more likely to accept a military presence on the streets in the event of austerity-related civil disturbances or public strikes.

However, the role of the military in the Olympics was far greater than this. The Guardian newspaper stated that, 'The Olympics have become a festival of the global security industry, with a running and jumping contest as a sideshow.'4 13,500 military personnel had been planned for security roles from the start, naval ships were stationed on the Thames and in Weymouth Bay, and Typhoon jets were based in London for the first time since the Second World War. Also installed were helicopters, sonic weapons, snipers, ground-to-air missiles (at six sites, including on residential buildings), and armed police on the public transport system. Armed Forces personnel participated prominently in the ceremonial events. Although community campaigns against the missiles failed to reverse the decision, the publicity around it did uncover just how militarised modern-day Olympics, and other mega-events, have become.

The military's agenda in schools

The 'engagement' of the armed forces with young people in schools is part of a wider, sophisticated recruitment strategy involving social media, computer games, clubs for teenagers to join, advertisement campaigns and contact within communities and schools. It is centred around the individual and their desire for positive challenges, adventure, a stable career, and to better themselves. The brief for one public relations campaign was 'self-development powered by the army'. What this actually means for a young person was encapsulated by the head of army recruitment strategy Colonel David Allfrey in 2007: 'Our new model is about

School resources and information on Camo Day and Armed Forces Day. The section on 'Real Life Heroes' in the army's Armed Forces Day teaching resource for 7-11 year olds suggests getting the children to look at various websites with information different roles within the military 'to see how the qualities you identified for being a hero apply to working for the Armed Forces to keeping our nation safe'. (credit – Emma Sangster)

raising awareness, and that takes a ten-year span. It starts with a seven-year-old boy seeing a parachutist at an air show and thinking, 'That looks great.' From then the army is trying to build interest by drip, drip, drip.'[5]

The UK Armed Forces visit thousands of schools each year. They offer school presentation teams, 'careers advisers', lessons plans, away days, one-to-one mentoring, interviews, and more. Across the country, they visit around 8,800 schools each year engaging approximately 900,000 students.[6] The education system is an important arena for access to young people as it offers an opportunity to reach a large proportion of children, and bypasses parents and other gatekeepers.

While the Armed Forces claim that their activity in schools is is not recruitment, the Ministry of Defence itself states that the access they are given enables them to 'provide positive information to influence future opinion formers, and to enable recruiters to access the school environments.'[7] The Ministry of Defence have also stated that curricular activities are 'a powerful way to facilitate recruitment'.[8]

The Ministry of Defence 2011 Youth Engagement Review identifies a third outcome in addition to the defence outcomes of raising awareness and providing opportunities for recruitment – personal and social development – and recognises that fits in well with the government's agendas in other policy areas.[9]

So, whilst the UK military do not actually sign any students up within schools, it is clear that their agenda is the long-term recruitment of young people into the Armed Forces - both as supporters of the military and, for some, actual enlistment (either when they leave school at 16, or later).

Militarising education at the national policy level

Up until recently, most Armed Forces activity in schools was coordinated at a local level, between individual schools and recruitment units or cadet associations. However, military-led activities are now being integrated into national education policy on the assumption that military approaches can provide a solution to social problems. The Department for Education's 'military skills and ethos programme' encompasses expanding Cadet forces in state schools, the Troops to Teachers programme, and the cadet version of National Citizen Service; also, developing academies and free schools run by ex-military personnel or sponsored by military institutions, and 'alternative provision' with a military ethos.[10]

Alternative provision includes the Military to Mentors programme run by Skillforce, and schemes for 'pupils who are either disengaged with education or at risk of becoming disengaged ....utilising the skills of a high proportion of former armed services personnel or other staff with experience in this field of work'. A number of these schemes, such as Commander Joe's and Challenger Troop, have been set up. They work in partnership with local authorities and schools to replace school-based learning with military-style activities in uniform.

The Department for Education states that 'We associate the military with many positive values, loyalty, resilience, courage and teamwork to name but a few. We recognise that these core values, together adding up to the 'military ethos' can also have a positive impact on pupils.' However, this does not explain why a military framework will develop these skills more effectively than one based in other 'service' contexts. Is it what Michael Gove, the Secretary of State for Eduction, has called the 'spirit of service' that he is keen to instil? Or is it in fact an ideological conception of the 'military spirit' that taps into political notions of Britishness and nationalism? Furthermore, the possibility that there may be aspects of a 'military ethos' that are not appropriate in education does not seem to have been considered. The military operate, after all, within a framework of conflict, and killing (if deemed necessary) is the reality of its business.

Two proposals which were put forward by right-wing think tanks are being encouraged by the government. The Centre for Policy Studies has proposed the establishment of free schools run entirely by ex-military staff. With a 'zero-tolerance' approach to discipline, the head teacher of one prospective free school stated that it 'will discard moral relativism and child-centred educational theory. "Self-esteem" training is out.... Competition...is in.'[11] The think tank ResPublica is advocating the development of military-sponsored academies, 'officially backed by the Armed Services and delivered by the Cadet Associations'.[12] The Department for Education is currently looking to establish free schools and academies that would be run or sponsored by the military in this way.

The 'military skills and ethos' initiatives conveniently deal with a number of government concerns: they would provide ex-Armed Forces personnel with employment opportunities; they introduce an ethos based on rigid discipline which returns to a more traditional approach in line with the current government's ideology around education; and they increase the opportunities for young people to be recruited, particularly to the reserve forces. The ResPublica report described how military academies would reverse widespread 'social educational failure' over generations, using the 2011 riots to suggest that certain communities were particularly dysfunctional. Their conclusion, entitled 'Revitalising the reserves, rescuing the young, helping society', makes it clear that the need of the country to increase its pool of reserve forces is key to this education policy. Politicians from left and right who support the programme speak almost exclusively from the perspective of providing young people with life skills and opportunities, without reference to other agendas that are driving the policy. The NASUWT, the largest teaching union in the UK, has referred to the idea of military academies as 'national service for the poor'.

The educational framework

One of the characteristics of the Armed Forces' involvement in UK education establishments up until now is that their relationships with schools have been informally established, unlike in the US where the military have a legal right to visit schools. This suggests that schools have the ability to choose whether they invite the Armed Forces in or not. As initiatives to promote the military in society proliferate more generally, it is unsurprising that schools accept the Armed Forces' offer (to run activities and provide resources for their pupils) enthusiastically.

However, there is a legal framework to ensure balance and guard against political indoctrination. In particular, section 407 of the Education Act 1996 states that when discussing political issues students must be 'offered a balanced presentation of opposing views'. Developing a shared understanding that information presented by the military comes from a one-sided perspective, driven by the military's own agenda, and that alternative points of view need to be made available to young people, is a vital step towards ensuring an ethical and legal balance.

Schools are also legally required under the Children's Act 1989 to act in loco parentis, assuming a duty of care for children and acting as a 'reasonable parent'. Surely a reasonable parent would present a balanced picture to a child in their care and ensure they are provided with an understanding that allows them to make an informed choice about decisions that will affect the rest of their lives.

The education system in the UK is rapidly changing. Many schools have become academies and they, and the free schools introduced by the current government, operate outside the control of the local education authority. The Department for Education is pursuing an aggressive policy of forcing other schools to become academies if they are deemed to be failing. With the introduction of military-led activities and approaches into national education policy, we may see the removal of the element of choice that schools currently have over whether or not they gives the Armed Forces access to young people on their premises. It is not clear if any young people will be forced to take part in military-led activities and what the consequences of this would be, and it remains to be seen what the impact of promoting the military within education will be for this generation of children. What is clear, however, is that for the foreseeable future, there will be more military activities within education, and that the task of challenging this will increase.

Notes

1 Quentin Davies, Bill Clark and Martin Sharp, 'Report of Enquiry into National Recognition of our Armed Forces', May 2008. [Online at www.ppu.org.uk/militarism/recognition_of_our _armed_forces.pdf (accessed February 2013)].
2 Hew Strachan, Tanya Armour, Pamela Healy, and Melissa Smith, 'Report of the Task Force on the Military Covenant', September 2010. [Online at www.gov.uk/government/uploads/system/uploads/attachment_data/file/27393/militarycove nanttaskforcerpt.pdf (accessed February 2013)].
3 MoD, 'Future Reserves 2020: Delivering the Nation's Security Together', November 2012. <www.official-documents.gov.uk/document/cm84/8475/8475.pdf> (accessed February 2013).
4 Simon Jenkins, '2012 Olympics: Kabul. Baghdad. London. Three to avoid this summer', The Guardian, 3 May 2012. <www.guardian.co.uk/commentisfree/2012/may/03/olympics-2012-kabul-baghdad-london-avoid> (accessed February 2013).
5 Stephen Armstrong, 'Britain's Child army', New Statesman, 5 February 2007. <www.newstatesman.com/politics/2007/02/british-army-recruitment-iraq> (accessed February 2013).
6 MoD, 'Engagement with UK schools', 2007; 'Supplementary Memorandum from the Ministry of Defence', in House of Commons Defence Committee, Recruiting and Retaining Armed Forces Personnel, Fourteenth Report of Session, 2007-08.
7 MoD, 'Engagement with UK schools'.
8 Directorate of Reserve Forces and Cadets, 'Strategy for Delivery of MOD Youth

Initiatives', 2005.

9   James Plastow, 'Youth Engagement Review: Final Report', December 2011. <www.gov.uk/government/publications/youth-engagement-review> (accessed February 2013).

10 See www.education.gov.uk/childrenandyoungpeople/youngpeople/militaryethos (accessed February 2013).

11 Tom Burkard, 'Red tape is delaying the foundation of a Free School staffed by ex-military teachers', *conservativehome*, 3 September 2011. <http://conservativehome.blogs.com/pla tform/2011/09/tom-burkard-troops-in-our-schools-will-do-more-than-troops-on-our-streets.html> (accessed February 2013).

12 Phillip Blond and Patricia Kaszynska, 'Military Academies: Tackling disadvantage, improving ethos and changing outcome, 11 January 2012. [Online at www.respublica.org.uk/documents/jnw_ResPublica%20Military%20Academies.pdf (accessed February 2013)].

Gender and Queer Perspectives

Survey findings - Gender and sexuality

Of the thirty-two countries surveyed, there is only an active attempt to recruit LGBT people in four. Eight countries don't allow LGBT people to enlist at all, although of those, Kenya is the only one where homosexuality is actually illegal. In Turkey men can be exempted from military service if they can 'prove' (including by providing photos or video footage of them having sex with men) that they are homosexual. But in the majority of countries, sexuality is simply not a recruitment criterion.

The widely-promoted values that the military is believed to imbue are invariably related to ideals of gender. In Finland, Russia, and Switzerland it is emphasised that military service makes you become a man; in France you are said to become yourself. In Spain, equality for women is stressed. India is the only country where there is no active attempt to enlist women. However, in India, like in the UK, although women can not officially be in front-line combat positions, they can still engage in combat.

In eleven countries the enlistment of both women and LGBT is presented as part of the 'morality' of the military by promoting equal opportunities: in ten only the enlistment of women is presented in this positive way, and in the remaining eleven this argument is not used at all.

Israel, Sweden, Colombia and the US are the only countries in which women and LGBT enlistment is both allowed (including combat), promoted specifically, and used as a public relations tool of the army's moral standards. It is interesting to see how this is used differently and for different social and political reasons in each of these countries, when in Colombia the enlistment of LGBT is often seen as a way to 'make them normal', whereas in the US the decision was part of a lengthy internal political debate, and in Sweden and Israel the enlistment of both women and LGBT is emphasised as a moral standard as opposed to the societies these countries are involved in combat with (in Sweden versus the Afghan oppression of women, and in Israel versus conservative-Islamic values in general).

Quotes from WRI's Countering the Militarisation of Youth conference

The image of masculinity...the model men that go to war, that compete. - Jorge Veléz, Colombia

The Ministry of Women, for example, was created in 2006 and since then one of the main goals that the Minister for Women has proposed is to provide two million female members to the militia. She has already set in motion a first stage where she promised 150,000... - Rafael Uzcategui, Venezuela

We do also have women in the military, but comparatively the ratio is low. – Samuel Koduh, Ghana

I remember one time a mission taking supplies to an orphanage. As a sergeant I was team-leader, and one of the soldiers in my unit said to me and my friend Elizabeth "You guys must be so proud to be able to give such a good image of women, 'cause the women here are so oppressed". - Kelly Dougherty, USA

Queer and gender critiques of military recruitment and militarisation

Andreas Speck

The military uses equality talk in its recruitment campaigns, which so often focus on young people. Given that far more young people encounter these recruitment campaigns than join the armed forces, the impact of this representation is broad. I write this from the perspective of a gay man, although despite not being very involved in the queer movement I identify with queer concepts rather than with a gay identity.[1] This is partly based on my own experience in the gay community, where the wish to be 'normal' and 'accepted' is common: this involves embracing our militarist society as it is. As an antimilitarist, anarchist, and feminist, I often felt uncomfortable with this. However, I often also felt that the antimilitarist movement is not very welcoming to queer or transgender people, and even though I did not experience open homophobia, I do think there is an assumption – at least by men – that one is straight.[2] Sexuality is not seen as an important aspect of the antimilitarist struggle, but I do think it is.

Militarism, Masculinity, and Heteronormatism

That militarism and masculinity are closely linked is obvious, and not only because soldiers are predominantly men. Nevertheless, I want to highlight some pertinent points. Firstly, while the military is clearly a masculine institution, this does not mean that there is only one form of military masculinity. Any modern armed force will require different forms of military masculinity, although they are not necessarily equally valued, nor recognised by the public. The dominant – or hegemonic – forms of military masculinity are probably still very close to the Rambo warrior image. This is mainly associated with ground combat troops, even though they may form a minority within the military. However, other forms of military masculinity based more on technology are playing an increasingly important role. Secondly, the public image of all these masculinities is heterosexual. Even militaries that allow queer people to serve represent themselves as straight in the mainstream media.

Gender, sexuality and recruitment

When we talk about military recruitment, it is important to do so from a queer and gender perspective. This doesn't just mean having an awareness of the military's efforts to recruit women, queer people, and other minorities; we also need to look at how the military's recruitment efforts make use of perceptions of gender and sexuality, and how at the same time they contribute to the social construction of gender and sexuality. The military doesn't just use certain images of masculinity to attract certain kinds of men; it also shapes masculinities, and therefore contributes to the everyday re-enactment of patriarchy and heterosexism.

According to the academic Melissa T Brown, the US military is still using masculinity as a focus in its recruitment efforts, using 'several versions of masculinity, including both transformed models that are gaining dominance in the civilian sector, and traditional warrior forms that can appeal to those who are threatened by the changes and looking for a refuge'.[3] Brown points out that the marines in particular continue to rely on a traditional warrior image, but that the other services also still emphasise masculine attributes, even when using economic benefits to attract recruits: 'the kinds of jobs a man can build a world of his own on' - not a woman. The situation in the UK appears to be similar.[4]

While in most countries conscription was or is (with the exception of Israel and Eritrea) only for men, armed forces' volunteer positions are often open to women. But this does not mean the military presents itself as less masculine. As Brown points out:

> The end of male conscription made the connection between masculinity and soldiering less automatic, and the services could theoretically have attempted to de-gender service in recruiting materials, but instead they re-forged the link, constructing masculinity both in ways traditionally linked to warriorhood and in alternative forms.[5]

Women rarely feature in recruitment adverts, and usually they are pictured in different roles: they are only 'offered some limited access to characteristics and experiences that have generally been associated with men, like testing oneself, experiencing adventure, and having a career.'[6]

The attempts by the military to recruit women and queers are mainly due to two reasons: recruitment shortfalls - although less so in the current economic climate - and outside political pressure from civilian society. In quite a few countries, access for women and queers had to be fought for in the courts, and only when the military had lost the legal battle did it embrace equal opportunities, but without a change at heart.

I have my doubts about how much the military's engagement with the queer community, for examples its presence at gay pride events, is really about recruiting, or whether it is more about on the one hand militarising the queer community by creating acceptance for militarism and the recourse to military solutions, and on the other presenting a public image of a modern and open military in a democratic country. The latter objective is closely linked to how 'Muslim fundamentalism' is framed as the main threat and enemy: it forms part of the anti-Muslim propaganda, rather than being a reflection of a genuinely open military friendly to women and queers.

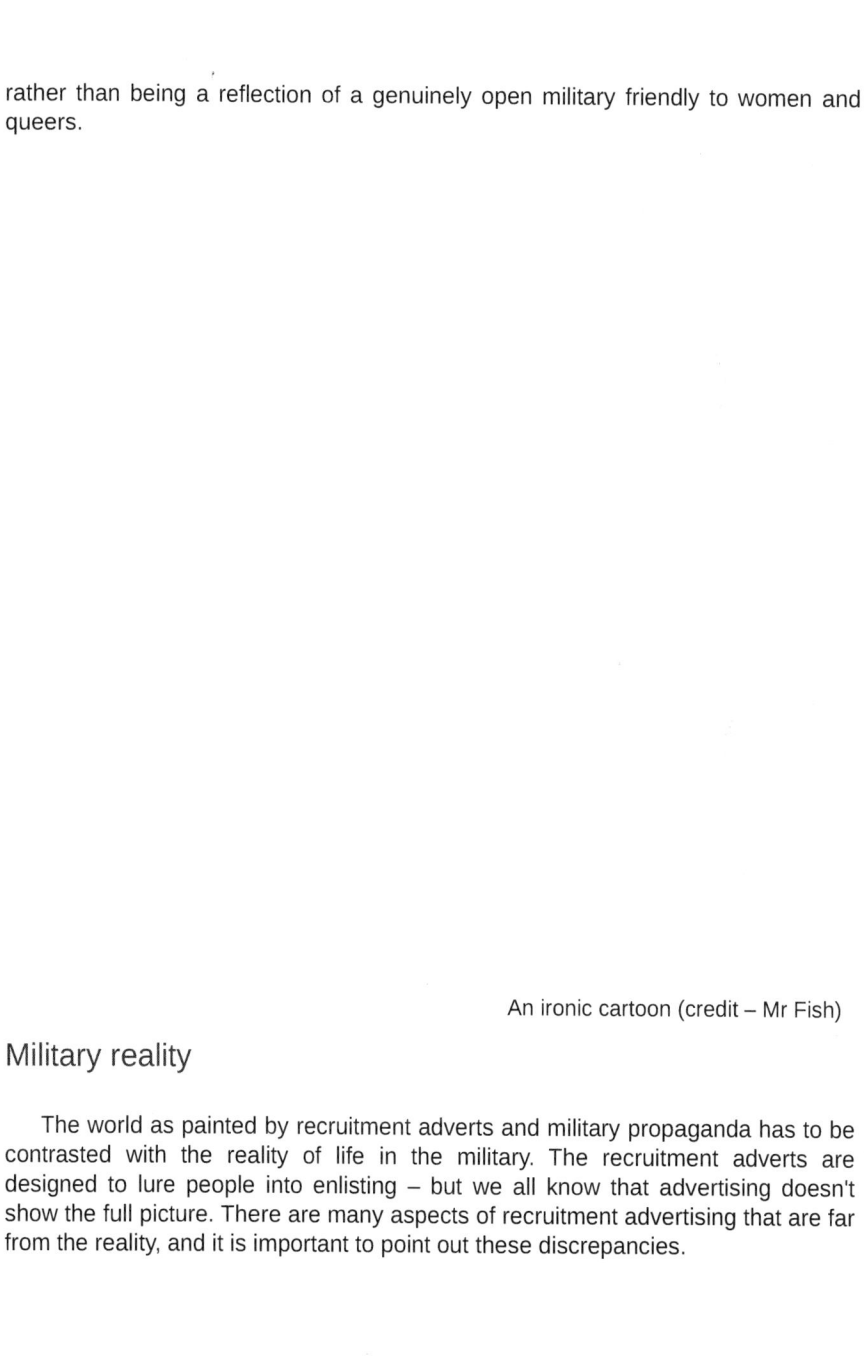

An ironic cartoon (credit – Mr Fish)

Military reality

The world as painted by recruitment adverts and military propaganda has to be contrasted with the reality of life in the military. The recruitment adverts are designed to lure people into enlisting – but we all know that advertising doesn't show the full picture. There are many aspects of recruitment advertising that are far from the reality, and it is important to point out these discrepancies.

Homophobia and sexual harassment

There are reports of homophobia in the armed forces of many countries, including those that do allow gays and lesbians to join – such as the UK, Germany and Canada - where studies have been conducted. In 2010, the ombudsman of the German Bundeswehr stated in his annual report that he again received complaints from soldiers who experienced discrimination based on their sexual orientation.[7] In the Canadian military, according to recent reports, homophobia including bullying is not unusual, but people don't report it unless it creates a toxic environment or is a serious threat.[8] Even though coming-out does not cause legal problems in these countries, it is not encouraged in a pre-dominantly straight masculine environment. As a result, diversity is not embraced, and sexuality is seen as a 'private matter'. There is similar anecdotal evidence from many other countries around the world, whether or not they allow lesbian or gays to serve.[9]

As the academic Victoria Basham points out with regards to the UK military, 'Privatising sexuality reinforces the heterosexist culture that made the previous policy (banning lesbians and gays from the military) possible in the first place'.[10]

For women in the UK military, sexual harassment is widespread. A 2006 study spaning three years, conducted by the Equal Opportunities Commission and the MoD showed that 99% of women in the armed forces had been exposed to sexual harassment, and 67% said it happened directly to them. 49% of reported cases lasted more than two months; 23% involved the victim suffering for more than twelve months.[11] This does not seem to have changed significantly since. A letter written on 25 October 2012 by the high ranking Major General John Lorimer to the Adjutant General Lieutenant General Gerry Berragan outlines a summary of Lorimer's views on equality and diversity (E&D) in the Army after speaking to 6,000 army personnel. Damingly, on sexual harassment, Maj Gen Lorimer states that 'every female officer or OR [other rank] that my Comd Sgt Maj has spoken to claims to have been the subject of unwanted sexual attention.'[12]

In the US military, according to official figures, 4.4% of women experienced 'unwanted sexual contact' – rape or sexual assault.[13] However, a 2003 study of women seeking health care through the Veteran's Administration from the period of the Vietnam war through the first Gulf War (1990-1) found that nearly one in three women was raped while serving - almost twice the rate of rape in general civil society - and that eight in ten had been sexually harassed.[14]

These statistics do not reveal the trauma nor the long-term consequences of the survivors of sexual harassment, assault, and rape.

The Canadian academic Gary Kinsman says that basic military principles and structure are at the root of heterosexist attitudes: the military has historically been a male-dominated, hierarchical and 'masculinist' institution. He claims that one product of a masculinist attitude is the association of male sexuality with extreme hostility, especially toward those men and women who don't fit in, including lesbians and gays: 'We're actually talking about very dangerous situations for women in general, but also for anyone who's openly identified as being queer, whether they are or not'.[15] Sexual harassment in the military serves a purpose: to show women that they don't belong in a male institution.

Hazing

Another part of the masculinist reality of the military is the hazing of new soldiers – often sexualised bullying and abuse, which forms part of the initiation, but can get much worse. While hazing is often associated with Eastern European or former Soviet militaries, where admittedly the scale of the problem is worse[16], it is also prevalent in Western armed forces. A Norwegian study found that 22% of soldiers reported having been hazed, and 19% that they had hazed others.[17] Hazing is also common in the British Army, as has been highlighted by several scandals in recent years. A 2003 survey found that 43% of respondents found bullying to be a problem, and 5% had been victims of it.[18]

However, hazing is not ordinary bullying. It forms part of regimental initiation rites, or, as the academic Hana Cervinkova put it in an article on Czech conscripts: 'a rite-of-passage, which involves psychological and physical violence perpetrated by the senior on the junior conscripts', and the humiliation of those to be initiated - their feminisation, including through sexualised violence and abuse.[19]

Hazing goes with masculinity. As the academic Elizabeth Allan points out:

> The more boys/men are fearful of being labelled as weak - the more likely they are to participate in hazing activities that are dangerous and even life-threatening... The predominant social construction of masculinity, and homophobia, work in tandem to create a climate in which violent and demeaning hazing practices are more likely to be tolerated and even considered beneficial for young men.[20]

Conclusion

Despite all the military's equality talk, and its inclusion of women and queer people, it remains essentially a masculine institution. Far from embracing diversity, it continues to promote itself as a man's world.

However, militarised masculinities, and the military's exploitation of equality talk in order to reach out to women and other sexual minorities, can be countered. The challenge is to acknowledge and condemn the discrimination of women, queer people and other minorities in the reality of the military, without falling into the trap of advocating a reform of the military rather than its elimination.

It is important to go back to the roots of queer liberation, which wasn't about equality within a patriarchal and militarist system, but a radical and fundamental change of our societies. Something got lost with the mainstreaming of gender and queer, and with equality talk; we need to reclaim that something. Our queer struggle is a struggle against all forms of power structures that press us into norms and binaries, of which the military is a major offender.

Notes

1   This article uses the term 'queer' because it is broader than lesbian, gay, bisexual and transsexual/transgender (lgbt). Queer has been reappropriated (or reclaimed) from its derogatory meaning by lgbt activists since the early 1990s and includes all those whose sexual orientation, activity, or gender representation places them outside the heterosexual mainstream with its gender and sexual binarisms.
2   Andreas Speck, 'Zwischen allen Stühlen? Schwul in der gewaltfreien Bewegung - gewaltfrei   in   der   Schwulenbewegung',   October   2000. <http://andreasspeck.info/de/node/26> (accessed 5 June 2012).
3   Melissa T Brown, 'Enlisting Masculinity: The Construction of Gender in US Military Recruiting Advertising and the Recruitment of the All-Volunteer Force' (Academic dissertation, 2007).
4   Melissa T Brown, '"Be the best": Military Recruiting and the Cultural Construction of Soldiering in Great Britain', *GSC Quarterly*, 5 (2002).
5   Brown, 'Enlisting Masculinity'.
6   Ibid.
7   Stern.de, 'Jahresbericht zur Bundeswehr: Mangel und Missstand an allen Fronten', 16 March 2010. <www.stern.de/politik/deutschland/jahresbericht-zur-bundeswehr-mangel-und-missstand-an-allen-fronten-1551308.html> (accessed 5 June 2012).
8   Andi Schwartz: 'Gay in the army. Despite years of inclusion, Canadian military still not a friendly   space   for   gays   and   lesbians',   23   February   2012. <http://www.xtra.ca/public/National/Gay_in_the_army-11576.aspx> (accessed 5 June 2012).
9   See, for example, from South Korea: The Korea Herald: 'Gay man's objection to service sheds   light   on   sexual   abuse   in   military',   16   December   2011. <http://view.koreaherald.com/kh/view.php?ud=20111216000668&cpv=0> (accessed 5 June 2012).
10 Victoria Basham, 'Harnessing Social Diversity in the British Armed Forces: The Limitations of 'Management' Approaches', *Commonwealth & Comparative Politics*, 47:4 (2009), pp. 411-429.
11 The Female Frontline, 'Sexual Harassment in the British Forces', 15 March 2012. <http://thefemalefrontline.wordpress.com/2012/03/15/199/> (accessed 5 June 2012).
12 Channel 4 News, 'Sexual harassment and bullying rife in the army', 28 November 2012. <http://www.channel4.com/news/sexual-harassment-and-bullying-rife-in-the-army> (accessed 14 May 2013).
13 Defense Manpower Data Center, 'Workplace and Gender Relations Survey of Active Duty Members', 2010. <www.sapr.mil/media/pdf/research/DMDC_2010_WGRA_Overview_Rep ort_of_Sexual_Assault.pdf> (accessed 5 June 2012).
14 H Patricia Hynes, 'Military Sexual Abuse: A Greater Menace Than Combat', *Truthout.org*, 26 January 2012. <http://truth-out.org/index.php?option=com_k2&view=item&id=6299:mili tary-sexual-abuse-a-greater-menace-than-combat> (accessed 5 June 2012).

15 Cited in Schwartz, 'Gay in the army'.
16 See, for example: Olga Miryasova, 'Abuse in the Military – Gender Aspects', August 2007. <www.wri-irg.org/node/6523> (accessed 5 June 2012).
17 Kristina Østvik & Floyd Rudmin, 'Bullying and Hazing Among Norwegian Army Soldiers: Two Studies of Prevalence, Context, and Cognition', *Military Psychology*, 13:1, (2001), pp. 17–39. <http://humiliationstudies.org/documents/RudminOstvikBullyingNorwegianArm y.pdf> (accessed 5 June 2012).
18 James K. Wither, 'Battling Bullying in the British Army', in Françoise Daucé and Elisabeth Sieca-Kozlowski (eds), *Dedovschina in the Post-Soviet Military*, (Stuttgart, 2006).
19 Hana Cervinkova, 'Time to Waste. Notes on the Culture of the Enlisted in the Professionalizing Czech Military', in Daucé and Sieca-Kozlowski, *Dedovschina*, pp. 205 – 220.
20 Elizabeth J. Allan, 'Hazing and the Making of Men', 2003. <www.stophazing.org/makingofmen.htm> (accessed 5 June 2012).

'One of the boys': the conscription of young women to the Israeli military

Sahar Vardi

Israel has had, since its creation, mandatory military service for both men and women. It prides itself, both internally and externally, on its relatively gender-equal military in which women can both contribute to their society just as men can, and get an opportunity to prove their worth. The apparent gender equality presented by the military provokes a particular feminist perspective on the conscription of women.

One could assume that in a country with compulsory conscription, convincing young people about the importance of – and their personal interest in – serving in the military is unnecessary. Yet in fact, in Israel, like many conscript societies, the promotion of the military and of the enlistment of young people happens in a variety of ways.

When I was about eleven or twelve my brother had a poster in his room of a female combat soldier in training, carrying a male soldier on her back, simulating an evacuation of an injured comrade in battle. At the time I made up my mind that I wanted to be a combat soldier; I wanted to prove to the men, but maybe more so to myself, that I could do the same things as them. The girl in the poster seemed to prove that. At more or less at the same age I also knew that I was against the Israeli military occupation of the Palestinians - that violence was not something that I would like to promote in any way. But the appeal of having an opportunity to really prove myself as equal to men in this very male-dominated field was stronger. With time, I grew out of this, as my understanding of feminism and equality developed. There are still times, however, when on an emotional level I get the same feelings, and sense the same admiration (maybe even envy) towards those women combat soldiers 'taking on' the men.

Historically, the heroisation of combatants has usually overlooked women. While feminist and anti-militarism movements tried to challenge the concept of heroisation, it seems the Israeli military has tried to promote participation of women in combat, at least for appearances. The conscription of women to the Israeli military is not only another part of universal conscription in Israel – and of the sentiment that 'everyone goes' – but is also specifically highlighted as a policy based on, and promoting, gender-equality. An official Israeli Defence Force (IDF) video from 2009 on the involvement of women expresses the same sentiment - that women can be equal to men if they join.[1]

An article from the mainstream Israeli news website Mako entitled '50 things you didn't know about the Israeli Defense Force [IDF]'[2], written by a female reporter, reveals:

- Israel is the only country in the world with mandatory military service for women.[3] Today women make 34% of the military, and 88% of the roles are open to them. A quarter of the officers in the IDF are women.

- In the past women were not allowed to serve on navy ships, but during the last sailors' training course the status of 'excellent sailor' was given to a woman.

- Karakal regiment is the only mixed regiment in the IDF, and both men and women combatants serve in it. There are no exceptions: the girls do Basic Training 07 (combat training), and carry MAG and Negev machine guns, and stretchers, just like any [male] combatant in the IDF.

Young female IDF field intelligence soldiers, 2011 (credit – Israel Defence Forces)

This illusion of equality has two purposes. The first is to motivate young women to serve, showing them that the military is a place for them to prove that they can be equal to men in their duties and performance. The fact that hundreds of soldiers complain about sexual harassment in the military every year, and, according to military research in 2002, 80% of female soldiers were sexually harassed during their service, somehow does not make it into the top 50.

The second purpose of this illusion of equality is part of the legitimisation of the military, for itself as well as for the rest of Israeli society and the international community. The Israeli military prides itself on being 'the most moral military in the world'.[4] This phrase is especially used to legitimise the IDF during combat, saying that because Israeli soldiers act in the most moral way possible considering the circumstances, the civilian casualties, injuries and damage to property during 'military operations', must be justifiable. After the attack on Gaza in 2009 (Operation Cast Lead) the then-Israeli Minister of Defence Ehud Barak responded to testimonies by soldiers regarding the harm caused to civilians by asserting:

> We have the most moral military in the world. I spent tens of years in uniform, I know what happened in Yugoslavia, in Afghanistan and in Iraq, and I tell you that from the chief of staff until the last soldier, the most moral military in the world stands at the disposal of the Israeli government. I have no doubt every specific incident will be looked into.[5]

But to maintain this perception, the IDF must appear to have a higher moral standard than that of the people it fights against, not only on the front line but also at the level of its core values. For this reason, the conscription of women and the illusion of equality for women inside the military system, together with the conscription of homosexuals and bisexuals, give the IDF the moral highground – when it comes to 'Western' values – compared to any other military in the world, and especially in the Middle East. And so the Israeli military and Israeli society can celebrate the compulsory conscription of woman as a progressive next step for women's liberation.

The other side of this is that the women's peace movement in Israel has been a dominant voice in the general peace movement for decades, and has managed to use their unique voice as women to influence policies. Interestingly, at times this was also done by using a role which such a militaristic society allowed women to dominate – that of a caring mother of a soldier – to demand the end of war and the return home of the soldiers. This strategy was employed effectively by the movement 'Four Mothers', which was instrumental in the final retreat of Israeli from Lebanon in 2000.[6] Other feminist peace movements took a different path, questioning the role given to them as supporters and educators of future soldiers, and formed groups such as Women in Black, New Profile, the Coalition of Women for Peace and many more, all trying to give a clear, ongoing feminist voice against the occupation and the militarisation of Israeli society.

In 2005 Idan Halili, a nineteen-year-old Israeli woman, declared her refusal to serve in the military saying:

> A strongly patriarchal institution, like the army, underlines female marginality and the superiority of male-identified values. ... It might be said that a mood of sexual harassment is endemic in the army. And so the demand that a woman enlist is tantamount to demanding that she cope with sexual harassment. I as a feminist, feel I must avoid military service and act to limit and reduce the influence of the army on civic society.

Today, we members of Israeli feminist movements working towards the demilitarisation of Israeli society must constantly provide a feminist alternative voice, both underlining the inherent patriarchy in the military and its effect on women, as well as presenting our alternative – a feminist voice for peace.

Notes

1   CNN, 'Israeli Army', 17 September 2009. <www.youtube.com/watch?v=Joh1NkEfqJ4> (accessed September 2012).
2   Hadas Duvdevani, '50 things you didn't know about the IDF', *Mako*, 3 June 2012. <www.mako.co.il/pzm-magazine/Article-c07be6a8371b731006.htm>(accessed September 2012).
3   In fact Eritrea has it too.
4   This phrase has been repeated by numerous Israeli politicians and generals, including, in recent years: former Prime Minister and Minister of Defence Ehud Barak, former military Chief of Staff Gabi Ashkenazi, former Prime Minister Ehud Olmert and many more.
5   Shahar Ilan and Fadi Iadath, 'Barak: we have the most moral military, every incident will be investigated', *Haaretz News*, 20 March 2009. <www.haaretz.co.il/news/politics/1.1251460> (accessed September 2012).
6   Four Mothers: www.4mothers.org.il/peilut/backgrou.htm (accessed September 2012).

Resistance

Quotes from WRI's Countering the Militarisation of Youth conference

I as Director of the Vocational Training Centre for former Child Soldiers implemented programmes for UNICEF including how to get children who were caught up in the war back into the mainstream of life – to get them back into school or vocational activities...Reduce or eliminate all sort of inequalities and violence will be reduced. If there is no violence, there would be no need for child soldiers... - Domino Frank Suleiman, Liberia

Talking in schools is a big part of what a lot of people do... giving young people a different perspective so they don't join the army...my experience talking to high school students is really positive: it's been very interesting to see how much they are shocked about my experience in Iraq. - Kelly Dougherty, USA

At Ceasefire we run nonviolence courses that we encourage young people and community leaders to participate in to see that this is the way in which they can resolve conflicts, whether with their neighbours, neighbouring countries, other bodies internationally. We feel that if we can give these essential tools to individuals...the military wouldn't be necessary...we do a lot of workshops in communities, a lot of awareness campaigns, we try to show films so that the young people can actually observe the many effects that militarisation comes with...we try to penetrate the military's media image, to say they are not really who they say they are. - Kaizer Tshehla, South Africa

I'm from a group called World Without War, and we are the only group that's supporting "political" conscientious objectors in South Korea...for the last ten years we've been focusing on introducing genuine alternative service [the current one involves four weeks of military training]. - Garam Jang, South Korea

In the town of Zwolle, there were good actions for years. Activists dressed as clowns satirically exposed the military structure. The clowns were always quickly arrested though. Last time the police rang the coordinator of the protest on the morning before the pledge to ask her how many people would be present. That evening the military show took place in the barracks instead of the city centre – this was a great success...I give lessons on peace in schools. I visit around 150 primary and secondary schools per year. The aim is to make children curious about conflicts, in order to show them how the concept of the enemy arises. At the end they should understand that in the long term conflicts are best solved without violence. The children have for the most part shown a keen interest and I have often had the impression that after the lesson on peace none of the pupils will be joining the army. That's obviously great. But the children have to think through this experience for themselves. - Geart Bosma, Netherlands

I had a Peace Studies education, to help me to be able to influence the combatants – to find out what is it that's pushed them to do that. In other words to identify their goals, and sort out which ones are legitimate, and which ones are not legitimate, and then the contradiction between the two parties who are involved in these conflicts, and maybe contribute to bringing about peace between them. - Samuel Koduh, Ghana

We also promote and give support to those who are in the reserves – after military service. The military can call you up again for a couple of days to practise – we give help and promote the notion that after you have done the military service you can still be a conscientious objector: you do five days of alternative service. Then you're completely freed from the military. - Paavo Kolttola, Finland

New Profile assists young people who want to get out of the military for whatever reason, runs youth groups that give a safe space to talk about the army – out of that grows critical thinking – and has an exhibition that shows militarisation – because for Israelis symbols of the military in ordinary life are invisible – which constructs some debates. If you take my parent's generation, then everyone went to the military – there wasn't such a thing as people who didn't serve. And then in my generation you have 12% getting out on mental health, which is very high. And I think that beyond the fact that it will mean less people in the military, which is already good, people that don't serve can allow themselves a different perspective on things, 'cause they're not part of the military system. - Sahar Vardi, Israel

When military recruiters have been at job fairs we've done different kinds of action: just standing outside handing out our own leaflets, or coming there as the Clown Army and trying to be recruited as clowns, or trying to recruit to the Clown Army. And also because the target group for the military is 15 to 25-year olds we go to high schools and talk about war and militarism and militarisation and the military...Of course it's up to everyone to decide what they want to do with their life, but we give people information about what the military really is doing. And in one of the classes we gave a workshop to, in the evaluation one person said "My thought was to join the military when I finish school, and now I've changed my mind". - Cattis Laska, Sweden

ForcesWatch tries to challenge the state and the Armed Forces on the ethics of the way they recruit young people, and also challenge this uncritical national pride in the Armed Forces. I also run a website called beforeyousignup.info, that presents the cons as well as the pros of joining the armed forces. And the Child Soldiers coalition is involved in lobbying: last year we actually managed to persuade the government to change the law so that all under-18s in the Armed Forces have a legal right to leave. They didn't have that before. Some school students have challenged army recruiters when they come in and some of them have actually chased them out of the building. There are actions around recruiting offices – close them down by occupying them, or handing out leaflets outside – and at parades and village fêtes, to give an alternative view. - David Gee, UK

Veterans for Peace UK was set up in 2011. Whereas in the US there's a culture where it's possible for veterans to question the wars in Iraq and Afghanistan, in the UK there are only a tiny handful who have spoken out. It's seen as a betrayal by soldiers to do that, so it takes a lot of courage. But there's a huge potential for it. And the only way the UK movement questioning military recruitment is going to take off and grow as it needs to and should do, is if more veterans are willing to make that stand. Which means it's our job to recognise the barriers they face and to support them. - David Gee, UK

The role of military veterans and current service members

Kelly Dougherty

As long as there have been wars and the military, soldiers around the world have resisted, deserted, and refused combat duty for both moral and political reasons, and civilians have supported them. From the formation of the St. Patrick's Battalion made up of soldiers who deserted the U.S. Army to join forces with the Mexicans during the Mexican-American War, to the Bonus Army in the 1930's where thousands of U.S. veterans marched and occupied Washington DC demanding back-pay for their service in World War I, to the huge GI[1] resistance movement during the Vietnam war, the United States has a rich and varied legacy of military members refusing to be used by their government to further political and economic agendas. GIs are the work force that make war and military occupation possible and, as such, have a critical role to play as leaders in the struggle to end war and militarism.

Veterans and military service members bring unique perspectives and important experiences and knowledge to organising work aimed at countering war and militarism. They have an inside perspective on the military mindset and culture as well as first-hand experience with the day-to-day realities of war and occupation. In countries that are waging foreign wars, such as the United States, military members and their families are the part of the population most clearly and immediately impacted by those wars. Being the most affected and having the first-hand experience that they do, many GIs become disillusioned with the military and political rhetoric and are radicalised by their experience. These men and women are perfectly suited to challenge the stereotypes of war, the myth that war is heroic, and the wide-held belief that a sense of duty and patriotism should override any personal, moral or political considerations. Often, people who haven't served in the military are reluctant to criticize the military for fear of appearing to be against the troops. When a veteran who has taken part in war tells their story and calls war out for the violent, corrupt, dehumanising sham that it is, it inspires and encourages both civilians and other veterans to voice their similar beliefs and lets them know that they are not alone. Service members and veterans are also well suited to challenge civilians to confront their own responsibility and complicity in the wars that their nation is waging. The soldier may be the bullet, so to speak, but the nation's population is the force aiming the gun. When men and women in the military withdraw their support for war and militarism, they have the potential to destabilize the entire system and shift the balance of power.

Having a network of non-military allies to support, work and learn with is essential for veterans and service members who are organising around issues of militarism. Many times, however, this is difficult. Civilians often don't know how to approach military people, and veterans often find it difficult to relate to people who are detached from the realities of war and military service. Many veterans want to move on and put their military experience behind them. A huge number of veterans are dealing with the often-debilitating effects of military trauma, including Post Traumatic Stress Disorder, traumatic brain injury, military sexual trauma, and other mental and physical wounds. They may struggle just to survive from one day to the next and are not healthy enough to participate in any additional activities, especially those that will force them to confront the traumatic experiences from which they are trying to heal.

Most veterans who want to become actively involved in anti-militarism have never been involved in organising and activism before and may bring a lot of enthusiasm, but little experience of and familiarity with the culture of social justice activism. This can cause the veteran to feel like an outsider, since they are unfamiliar with the norms, language and history of this specific sub-culture. Also, veterans often feel stereotyped, marginalized and tokenized by civilian activists. For example, in the early years of Iraq Veterans Against the War, our members were often asked to speak about their experiences in Iraq, but they were not asked to participate in the planning and organising of actions. This made many veterans feel like people in the anti-war movement were using them to validate their own legitimacy instead of considering them as equal participants. Experiences like these serve to further enforce an idea perpetuated in the military that civilians aren't to be trusted and that they will never understand or care about the sacrifices and experiences of soldiers. Conversely, civilian activists may be mistrustful of veterans and service members and angry with them because of their willing participation in war and occupation. For someone with experience organising in anti-oppression and anti-militarization circles, they may be shocked and offended by the often sexist, bigoted, and disrespectful attitudes that veterans may bring with them in their transition from soldier to activist. Civilian activists may be unsure of how to confront a veteran about offensive, unhealthy behaviour that is commonplace and normalized in military culture, as it often is in society at large.

In order to confront and overcome these obstacles to working together, civilians and veterans must approach one another with openness and the willingness and ability to listen to each other. This helps to build strong relationships where people can better learn from each other and create strong alliances and campaigns. Iraq Veterans Against the War works closely with veteran and non-military organizations and groups alike, including the Civilian Soldier Alliance, Veterans For Peace, Military Families Speak Out, Afghans For Peace, the Occupy movement, and various labour and human rights groups. Just as the veteran or service member brings crucial experience and perspective to organising work, the civilian often has a wealth of experience and their own unique connection to issues of war. People who have been involved in anti-militarism work have experience organising around social justice issues, building campaigns, can offer perspective and analysis of larger systems of oppression, and have historical knowledge of popular movements that have confronted systems of injustice. They may also have their own very personal connections to the devastating consequences of war and can share this perspective with the veteran.

These men and women can help to integrate the warrior back into society and encourage and facilitate positive and meaningful actions that can be very healing, empowering and reconciling for a veteran. As we narrow the divide between civilians and soldiers, it becomes easier to narrow the divide between anti-militarism issues and other issues dealing with exploitation and injustice, from environmental degradation to economic inequality. For example, the U.S. occupation of Iraq has everything to do with melting polar ice caps, economic austerity in Greece and sweatshop working conditions in Bangladesh. When we begin to see the commonalities linking our experiences and issues to those of other groups, we become better equipped to engage in the sort of transforming and organising that can dismantle systemic oppression.

The work of Iraq Veterans Against the War, in particular, has focused on withdrawing military support from the wars in Iraq and Afghanistan. IVAW was founded in 2004 by a group of Iraq veterans who returned from Iraq angry and disillusioned by their experiences and wanted to work with others to end the occupation. From its founding, IVAW has called for three things: the immediate withdrawal of all occupying forces from Iraq, full benefits for returning veterans, and reparations for the Iraqi people. Since 2009 IVAW has included withdrawal from Afghanistan and reparations for the Afghan people in these points of unity. Our organization has undergone much change and growth during the past eight years and we are currently undergoing an internal strategy process to assess how best to structure our organising work as we move forward.

One of the ways that IVAW members have worked to withdraw military support from the wars is to do counter recruiting, or 'truth in recruiting', work. Military recruiters at best give potential recruits a very one-sided view of military service. At worst, recruiters lie and mislead prospective recruits in the hope of getting more young men and women to enlist. For example, recruits will often be told by recruiters that they will not be deployed or, if they are, that they won't be on the 'front lines.' A recruiter can never guarantee where a person, once enlisted in the military, will serve and, in today's wars, there are no front lines and cooks can be killed just the same as infantrymen. Recruiters are given broad access to high school students and are present on many high school campuses. Many young people see joining the military as the only way of getting a job, earning money for college, or getting out of their town or out of a dangerous neighbourhood. Many IVAW members joined the military for these reasons and have experienced the lies and half-truths of military recruiters. Our experiences have shown us that the reality of military service is often unrecognisably different from the picture painted by recruiters, military advertising, and civilian perception.

Many veterans find it very rewarding to be able to offer young people a different viewpoint, one not influenced by the pressure to meet recruitment numbers. IVAW

IVAW group at Fleet Week San Francisco, 2012. Each year IVAW and their allies attend the event to talk with and give truth-in-recruitment materials to young people and their families there, and GI rights materials to active duty service members (credit - Siri Margerin)

members have spoken to students across the country, from elementary school students to university students. I've done this many times. The simple act of telling the story of your military experience, your experience in a war zone, and the difficulties you face when you come home and leave the military, can have a profound effect on young people who have never heard anyone talk about their military service outside of the patriotic, black and white lens of the military establishment. Speaking candidly about military realities to young people is a way for veterans to share viewpoints and perspectives that were never shared with them and it can mean the difference between deciding to join the military and deciding to choose another path.

IVAW uses the term 'truth in recruiting' to convey the sentiment that young men and women have a right to be well-informed of the risks and realities of military service. We've pressured high schools to let us set up counter recruiting tables to act as a balance to the heavy presence of military recruiters. We've collaborated with other organizations, such as the American Friends Service Committee, to create counter-recruitment videos and literature. We've organized actions at military recruiting centres to protest about misleading, dishonest recruiting practices. There are many ways to withdraw military support from the wars, and truth in recruiting is one way that many IVAW members find to be incredibly rewarding.

I was recently invited to speak with an Afghanistan veteran at a high school by two students and their teacher. The students were feeling frustrated that the only military speakers to come to their school had been unquestioningly pro-military and they had experienced a September 11th commemoration event that was hyper-nationalistic with no nuance or retrospection. They felt that their student body was being done a disservice and should be presented with alternative, critical viewpoints. Throughout the day, we spoke to the entire student body during an assembly and more in-depth to individual classes. We were able to have discussions, to challenge and be challenged, in a way that the students' never had with any of the other military centred speakers or events before. I've also spoken to elementary-school children about the Iraq war. This was a challenge because it's difficult to know the best way to speak to children about the violent realities of war and the military. One year, my Iraq veteran friend and I used a role-play activity to show what it might be like for the children to be the subject of a raid and search. We wanted to show the unfairness of targeting mass populations in a way that wasn't too scary or graphic. Since the Unites States is a very militarized country, we are taught at a young age to unquestioningly support the military and government and have simplistic myths about war reinforced on a daily basis. By offering young people, regardless of their age, an alternative perspective and story, we have an opportunity to make an impact that will foster critical thinking and encourage more people to challenge the militarism of our culture.

Over the past two years, IVAW, working closely with the Civilian Soldier Alliance, has focused on the Operation Recovery campaign, which focuses on the right of service members and veterans to heal from military trauma. This campaign is structured on the transforming, organising model, which seeks to not only win a specific gain, but to transform individuals and society through empowerment, an understanding of our humanity, and common human rights-based values. By focusing on an issue that many people can support, namely that service members who've been injured mentally or physically due to their military service should not be forced to redeploy to combat zones or otherwise engage in activities that further injure and traumatize them, we have the opportunity to address larger issues of militarism. Asserting your right to heal from trauma is often a revolutionary act for a service member to take. The military enforces the idea that your individual needs and concerns are irrelevant. What matters is following orders and doing what needs to be done to accomplish the mission, whatever your commanders or political figures decide that mission to be. You are a GI, a piece of government property to be used and abused as the military sees fit. If you're on your fifth combat tour and you have to ingest a handful of psychotropic drugs just to get out of bed and go on your patrol in Afghanistan, you're expected to do it for the sake of 'mission accomplishment' and 'the good of the nation'. If you've been raped by a man in your unit, you're expected to shut up about it and continue working as though nothing happened so you don't damage 'unit cohesion'. If you go to sick call to see a doctor because you're in physical or emotional pain, you're labelled as 'weak' and accused of faking illness in order to get out of doing your duty.

As the military dehumanizes its soldiers it creates an environment and mentality that makes it easier for the soldiers to dehumanize the people in the countries they are occupying and bombing. Asserting our right to heal is a way to assert our humanity and reject the violence of military culture. It allows us to talk about how being denied the right to heal is a human rights violation, how it is a symptom of a patriarchal, militaristic capitalist system that values the consolidation of wealth and power over all else and is, by its nature, destructive, oppressive, and maintained by systemic violence. We are working to not only gain changes in military policy, but to build a service member and veteran led movement that ends militarism by transforming ourselves, military culture and American society.

The militarism and violence that IVAW is organising to dismantle is not just an American phenomenon or U.S. problem. The hegemonic system that uses military force for economic and political gain is exploiting, oppressing, and killing people and ecosystems worldwide. People in communities across the world continue to resist this violence and destruction in whatever ways they can. For those of us focusing our energy on issues of militarism, it is essential to engage and involve the soldiers and veterans who have been an integral part of that system as they grow from being a cog in the machine to being a wrench in the machine, so to speak. When you realize that you've pointed a rifle in the face of a child or old woman so that a corporation could make a profit, that you've hated and dehumanized a whole group of people and that the experience has made you hate yourself, that you've compromised your own morals and values in order to be a good soldier and follow orders, you have an opportunity to use those experiences to expose the horrors of war and work with others to make positive changes.

Notes

1   'GI' is a term meaning 'Government Issue' that came into use in the US during World War I to refer to military personnel and their equipment. The term emphasises service members' status as pieces of property belonging to the government.

Child Rights: Using international law and the UN

Ralf Willinger

Human Rights organisations are increasingly using International law and the UN to draw public attention to human rights violations and to put pressure on the oppressors responsible. The civil peace movement can make use of these mechanisms for their purposes as well. One example at the level of international human rights law, is the UN Convention on the Rights of the Child; another is the UN Human Rights Council. In both cases there is a reporting mechanism to monitor states' compliance with their obligations under the Convention and implementation of the respective rights in which the participation of civil society is explicitly provided for.

There are several articles in the UN Convention on the Rights of the Child concerning topics particularly relevant to the militarisation of youth, such as article 19 (protection from violence), article 29 (aims of education, among them education in the spirit of understanding, peace, tolerance), and the fundamental principle of the Convention enshrined in article 3: that the best interests of the child should be a priority in relation to other interests, including state interests such as recruiting young people for the national armed forces. In addition, the Optional Protocol to the UN Convention on the Rights of the Child on the involvement of children in armed conflict, which is now ratified by 150 states, determines how states need to protect children affected by war.

State Reporting Procedure for the UN Convention on the Rights of the Child

The 193 Treaty Parties of the UN Convention on the Rights of the Child (all states except for the United States and Somalia) have to report approximately every five years on their compliance with the obligations under the Convention and the Optional Protocols. For this purpose, they ought to hand in a so-called State Report, which is made public. Subsequently, civil society organisations (NGOs) and individuals have the opportunity to draft their own reports, documents or other information (for example, films), pointing at deficiencies in the State Report and in the state's implementation of the Convention in general (so-called Shadow Reports or Alternative Reports).

The governments and the organisations involved will then be called for consultation meetings with the UN Committee of the Rights of the Child in Geneva, usually separately. There (or sometimes beforehand in writing) the Committee may request further data, case studies or other documents in order to gain a comprehensive view on the child rights situation in the respective country.

The UN Committee for the Rights of the Child is a body composed of independent, non-government experts from 18 different countries. These are often academics, NGO representatives or other child rights experts. In the final stage of the reporting procedure, the UN Committee drafts and publishes its Concluding Observations. These might be clear recommendations to the reporting state on specific ways to improve its implementation of child rights in the future. In the next round of reporting, approximately five years later, the state has to report on how it has implemented the specific recommendations given by the Committee.

Using the state reporting procedure to challenge the militarisation of youth

A concrete example of how NGOs can use the state reporting procedure to challenge the militarisation of youth is the Child Soldiers Shadow Report on Germany. The child rights organisation Terre des Hommes has, in cooperation with Kindernothilfe and other child rights and development organisations, published three of these Child Soldiers Shadow Reports: in 2007, 2011, and 2013. They were drafted by the jurist Hendrik Cremer and examine how Germany has complied with its obligations in relation to child soldiers under the Child Rights Convention and the Optional Protocol on the involvement of children in armed conflict. They were handed over to the UN Committee of the Rights of the Child in Geneva during the State Reporting Procedure for Germany.

In 2008, upon the finalisation of the last State Reporting Procedure on this Optional Protocol, the UN Committee advised Germany, amongst others, to raise the recruitment age for entry to the German armed forces to 18. Also, to improve the assistance and treatment of refugee children, and 'specifically prohibit the sale of arms when the final destination is a country where children are known to be - or may potentially be - recruited or used in hostilities.'[1]

Although the recommendations of the Committee as well as the Shadow Report Child Soldiers 2007 have been discussed several times in the German parliament and by the government, hardly any of the recommendations have yet been implemented. This is the reason why civil organisations continue to be active. The 2011 Shadow Report and the updated version of 2013 focus on three issues: the recruitment and promotion practices of the German national army targeted at minors (for instance, promotions in schools, youth media, fairs, and employment agencies), refugee children, and arms exports.

The oral consultations in the current State Reporting Procedure on Germany will have taken place during 2013, while the Concluding Observations of the Committee are expected to come out in early 2014. However, the points of criticism included in the Shadow Report, as well as the deficient German implementation of the recommendations of the UN Committee, will have already been widely discussed. Due to the fact that the Shadow Reports argue with international human rights law and recommendations of the UN and form part of the framework of the UN human rights system, they have a strong impact on both media and politics.

Furthermore, civil society protests against the insufficient situation of implementation, with campaigns such as Aktion Rote Hand (Red Hand Action), Schulfrei für die Bundeswehr (Armed Forces-free Schools), Jetzt erst Rechte für Flüchtlingskinder (Now more than ever: Rights for Refugee Children), and Aktion Aufschrei – Stoppt den Waffenhandel (Action Outcry – Stop the Arms Trade). The pressure on the German government to implement the recommendations of the UN Committee has thereby increased.[2]

Children in Congo marking Red Hand Day, February 12, when people around the world call on governments to act on child soldiers (credit – Coalition to Stop the Use of Child Soldiers)

Universal Periodic Review in the UN Human Rights Council

In the Universal Periodic Review procedure of the UN Human Rights Council there are similar options for civil society to be involved and express views. In this case, the relevant NGO can send reports directly to the Human Rights Council itself by emailing uprsubmissions@ohchr.org. The Member States of the Human Rights Council can bring up certain aspects of the points made, in the discussions of the Human Rights Council. This procedure similarly can exert pressure on the respective government and potentially result in an improvement of the human rights situation in that country.

The politics of military recruitment, conscientious objection to military service promotion, and the promotion of the military can all be addressed through both of these UN reporting procedures. They are effective mechanisms at both national and international level for political advocacy and increasing public pressure. An example of a major success in recent years is the raising of the minimum age of military recruitment in many states, including South Africa, Nepal, Italy, Spain, and Poland.

Notes

1   UN Committee on the Rights of the Child, 'Concluding Observations: Germany,' 1 February 2008.
2   Shadow Report Child Soldiers. <www.kindersoldaten.info>; Red Hand Day. <www.redhandday.org>; Action Outcry - Stop the Arms Trade. <www.aktion-aufschrei.de>; Campaign against Military Promotion in German schools (German only). <www.schulfrei-fuer-die-bundeswehr.de>; Campaign 'Now more than ever – Rights for Refugee Children' (German only). <www.jetzterstrechte.de> (all accessed February 2013).

Translated from the original German by Josephine Wragge and Ralf Willinger

Resisting the militarisation of education

Kai-Uwe Dosch, Sarah Roßa and Lena Sachs
(amalgamated by Michael Schulze von Glasser)

The militarisation of the education system in Germany

In Germany, hardly a week goes by without coming across 'Germany's heroes' in uniform. They grin from billboards, television screens, student magazines, and booklets on trains, advertising a 'career with a future'. The slogans 'In the line of duty for freedom' or 'We. Serve. Germany.' appear to be the mantras of a new militarisation: one that wishes to bring the population to a martial 'peace course'.

In schools, the German Armed Forces give lessons and impose their influence on the training and development of teachers. Military service counsellors are invited to schools to advertise the career possibilities in the armed forces, or to build their advertising playgrounds in the schoolyard (the so-called 'career meeting places'). The armed forces even have a say on the content of the school curriculum; they increasingly install youth officers in the schools: young, well-educated and rhetorically-trained soldiers who act the part for political education. The cooperation between schools and the armed forces, which has existed since the forces' foundation in 1955, reached a new height in 2008 and subsequently with the finalised 'cooperation agreements' in eight of Germany's sixteen federal states between the armed forces and the responsible Ministry of Education. This new involvement is hidden under the guise of political education, but serves as recruitment and the legitimisation of the policy to militarise security.

Resistance

This increasing cooperation between the armed forces and educational institutions has been closely monitored and questioned critically - many people who have actively challenged the militarisation of youth have done so in the field of education. Resistance to the militarisation of education varies between countries. In Germany there has been a debate on whether to focus on attaining the provision in state schools of the same amount of peace education as there is military education, or whether the military should be banned completely. The resistance against militarisation in Germany has noticeably gained strength since this 2008 'cooperation agreement': different organisations in five German states have combined to campaign or broaden alliances in order to take action against the intrusion of the armed forces in the educational system. There are now active groups and initiatives in all of these states that stand against the militarisation of schools by sending protest letters, producing fact sheets, doing presentations, holding discussions, rallies, and so on.

Along with this there are antimilitaristic groups, peace organisations, other groups like the large Education and Science Workers' Union, and the children's rights organisation Terre des Hommes. They have all made it clear that they oppose militarisation, for example by urging school administrations to ban the military, and by supporting students to be absent from military education sessions. Even individual student councils, parent representatives and youth organisations have taken a stand to deal with the problem and resist the involvement of the armed forces in schools. Activities range from public relations, discussion meetings, information booths, protest letters to the respective state governments, and the collection of signatures for petitions protesting against school visits by soldiers, to demonstrations and rallies. Concurrently, a number of information brochures and other materials on the topic have been produced. From 24 to 29 September 2012, a nationwide campaign Week of Action For Military-Free Education and Research took place, which linked numerous regional and local initiatives and saw actions in many towns and cities, including the handing out information on the negatives of joining the armed forces.

There have been some notable, if small, successes. In six schools nationwide, collaboration with the armed forces was rejected through the decision of the students or by a staff conference. These 'military-free schools' are pioneers - models for other schools that also wish to oppose the militarisation of their institution. Three of them were awarded the Aachen Peace Prize this year. Direct actions have also had results: the armed forces have been known to call off promotional events after some such protests. In the University of Education in Freiburg, an army event took place only with a massive police presence, following the online announcement of protests. As a result, Freiburg youth officers had to decline an invitation from the university's student council for an armed forces role play. At a vocational school in Hessen, a youth officer had to cancel a visit because of a critical questionnaire he was sent beforehand: his superiors no longer approved of the meeting. The armed forces are not at all immune to protests; they can be made to retreat.

Furthermore, thanks to the long-term commitment of critics of the military, cooperation agreements – for example in Saarland and North Rhine-Westphalia – have been stopped in their tracks. In North Rhine-Westphalia, soldiers have been excluded from the training of teachers. Additionally, there are continuing and intensified efforts in the peace movement against militarisation in schools, which have even included successfully pressurising the Ministry of Education and Cultural Affairs to issue favourable decrees. However, due to financial limitations, getting the same number of peace activists in schools as there are soldiers is unfeasible.

Despite the substantial public criticism of the militarisation of schools, many instructors and the school governing bodies do not see that there is a problem. In

A protest - with toy tanks, planes, soldiers and fake blood strewn on the floor - calling for the demilitarisation of Kassel University, May 2012 (credit - Michael Schulze von Glaßer)

addition, antimilitarists still often encounter a lack of public understanding on the issue. Although the movement against militarisation in educational institutions in Germany has had some successes, and more and more people are being won over to resistance, there is still much to be done. The present bold advertising approaches of the armed forces can only be countered by sustained and vigilant protest.

There should be several levels of action. Firstly, schools as a whole can be demilitarised through the provision of antimilitarist and peace education resources, a greater curricular emphasis on critical thinking, and more radically through the creation of democratic decision-making councils with students, parents, teachers, and other staff represented on them. Secondly, parents and students should be better informed about children's rights not to attend activities run by or associated with the military, and alternative activities – such as visits from children with experience of war, or visits to anti-war exhibitions – should be put on.

More information on the issues must be circulated, using different media, and the pressure on the state governments responsible for education policy must be increased. This should include direct action and civil disobedience, for example picket lines in front of military stalls at education exhibitions. It is also essential to place the protest against the militarisation of school students into a social context as a whole, for it is only the militarisation of the country's foreign and domestic policy that is forcing young people to become involved in war.

Antimilitarists and peace activists must move on confidently with clear arguments and demands to confront the militarisation of education and society, as well as the militarisation of political and economic policies, sharing their

Graffiti on the wall of a school in Berlin reading 'Military-free zone', March 2010
(credit - Michael Schulze von Glaßer)

experiences in order to maximise their effectiveness and move towards a world that is fundamentally peaceful and free of military domination.

Translated from the original German by Diana Vega

Direct Action against Militarism

based on a piece by Cecil Arndt

In different countries, war and militarisation take on very different meanings and have different effects, depending not only on the presence or absence of direct acts of war but also on country's political, economic, and social circumstances, and its history and traditions. As these factors define not only to the types, levels, and effects of militarisation but also the ways in which it can be effectively resisted, the scope of this article is inevitably limited; it can only provide a Western, European, largely German perspective on the use of direct action to oppose the militarisation of youth, although it explores possibilities in other countries nonetheless.

Militarisation, in whatever form it takes, must be understood as always being directed at young people. The militarisation of youth relies not only on their direct recruitment into the armed forces, but on the widely growing intrusion of the military into the lives and minds of people of all ages. This intrusion influences individual daily routines, preferences and choices, as well as general perceptions. The common theme is the normalising of war and the military.

For those living in places where the reality of war seems far away, the military presence in everyday life sometimes goes unnoticed. It can take forms such as cooperation with civil institutions such as Ministries of Education and Development and healthcare providers, musical entertainment, the out-sourcing military logistics to private economic partners, or the direct recruitment of young people in schools, job centres, and elsewhere.

In the Western world, from where wars are exported to places usually perceived as 'less developed', the ability to wage war very much depends on the population's support for the military, and thus on general assumptions about war and its normality. The strategies used to normalise war and the military, inducing a view of them as detached from their violent, destructive reality (at least in those countries where people are not directly affected by war), vary a lot from country to country, and so does resistance to them.

Taking direct action

Any direct action against war and militarisation should be seen as direct action against the militarisation of youth, in that it is unmistakeably aimed at demasking the supposed normality of war(fare), thus offering an alternative vision of a world without war and militaries, and highlighting the individual's possibility to choose to work towards this. Antimilitarist direct action does this by challenging general assumptions regarding authority and by undermining predominating, government-led expectations of socially accepted behaviour. Looked at in this way, direct action against the militarisation of the youth allows the reclaiming of the term 'humanitarian intervention', grounded in individuals' 'responsibility to protect' from (and act against) war and militarisation.

There is a rich variety of activist traditions and knowledge reaching back to at least the beginnings of the First World War – ranging from labour strikes to direct disarmament activities – and there is a wealth of creativity among contemporary activists when it comes to confronting new(er) forms of militarisation. Traditional forms of antimilitarist direct action, with precedents noted in brackets, include: the blockading of military bases (Faslane nuclear submarine, Scotland[1]) and military transports (Husum, Germany[2]); the sabotage of military planes (Shannon, Ireland[3]), naval vessels (Loch Goil, Scotland[4]) and military vehicles (Hanover, Germany[5]); the labelling of sites of war and militarism such as military weapons testing ranges (Luleå, Sweden[6]), city centres (London, UK[7]) or universities (Potsdam, Germany[8]), and the trespassing of military areas (NATO headquarters in Brussels, Belgium[9] and Letzlingen, Germany[10]).

More recent forms of action include: ironic parades to counter the armed forces' 'pink-washing' (promoting their supposed openness towards LGBT people, as in Sweden and Israel), 'die-ins' at events and festivals where military bands or exhibitions provide entertainment for the public (for example in Germany and Sweden), and the circulation of literature denouncing the growing normalisation of the military's influence on people's lives (such as in Spain).

Along with the growing militarisation of war-exporting Western countries there is a proliferation of the sites, events and institutions which can help activists to oppose the normalisation of war and militarism. For example, the growing number of recruitment events held by the armed forces at schools and job centres represent opportunities for causing disruption (using one or more of the approaches listed above), or undermining the military's unbalanced self-representation by depicting the negative side of war, for example by handing out leaflets, fake blood or instructions on how to make a coffin to any young people present, or by interrupting military officials' talks with challenging questions.[11]

International variation

While there have always been proud military parades in Great Britain, the appearance of the German armed forces at public events is a more recent development, given Germany's history. And while joining the military has always been presented as a good move for a young person's future in the US – including being a way to attain citizenship – in Sweden the emphasis is on adventure and sport, as seen with the text service which sends military fitness activity instructions.

However, militarisation processes always draw upon the construction of national identities, so good antimilitarist actions should try to highlight the issues of nationalism, racism, and constructions of the 'other'.

Sharing our experience and knowledge on taking direct action with activists from other countries and of different ages is not only inspirational, but can also help encourage us to try alternative approaches rather than sticking conservatively to what we are used to, which may hinder our impact. However, international variation must always be kept in mind. One important example is that laws and the implications of breaking them can differ greatly from country to country. While it is relatively easy to approach a member of the armed forces in a public place in Germany, for example, this may be life-threating in some other countries. While in Belgium activists entering the grounds of the NATO headquarters, or 'bombspotting' (the attempted inspection of nuclear weapons by civilians) at other military bases, have never been tried in court (due to officials' fear of the spotlight that public trials would put on these already-controversial issues), in most other places activists have to accept a high probability of being arrested and tried. And while activists in the UK who sabotaged military equipment such as planes and naval vessels have been found not guilty by juries who value the life-saving effects of the antimilitarist act more than any material damage it may have caused, antimilitarists in Germany can face many years of prison if found guilty of the same. In addition, individual activists have different personal circumstances, including their legal status, economic situation, health, and skills, which also inform what they are able to do.

International campaigns are a way of taking these differences into account while at the same time connecting activists. They not only offer the chance of mutual support but can also map different aspects and developments of war and militarisation and their effect on people. One example of successfully working together on an international level is the European campaign War Starts Here.[12] War Starts Here draws to people's attention, disrupts, and blocks the places, institutions, organisations and events in war-exporting countries that - in different, sometimes almost-imperceivable ways - are involved in warfare, including schools and universities where the military are involved through teaching and weapons research, to the military's use of public infrastructure such as railways, electronic communication facilities, and their participation at festivals and sports fixtures.

In focusing on mapping the presence and influence of the military within the societies of the war-exporting countries and calling for them to be highlighted, disrupted and blocked, War Starts Here also paves the way for joint activities across borders and political traditions. It offers a framework that allows participation and engagement with other activists that can also always be adjusted to suit individual and group preferences and needs.

Conclusion

The sharing of experience is a basic condition for widening the horizons and scopes of direct action against militarisation. It allows us to develop new perspectives and possibilities, and provides solidarity that transcends borders and politics. This requires work. The transfer of knowledge and skills from one generation to the next, and among activists with very different backgrounds, needs to be improved. This could be done by holding small meetings, or larger workshops or conferences.

The various types of direct action against militarisation have multiple effects: they directly counter recruitment to the armed forces, whilst at the same time offering an alternative vision of an unmilitarised world; any direct action against militarisation will perforce demonstrate the possibility of saying 'No!' to war and militarism and to the current relationships of power that drive them.

Notes

1 The Faslane Naval Base near Glasgow, as well as being the site of a long-running peace camp, has repeatedly been targeted by activists who have chained themselves to its gates, climbed the fences, entered the base by canoe, and disrupted the road transportation of the missile warheads.
2 In February 2008, activists blocked the train transport of equipment for the NATO Response Force by chaining themselves to the rails.
3 In 2003, activists entered Shannon airport and disarmed a US warplane with a mallet, poured human blood on the runway, and painting the hanger where the warplane was stationed.
4 In 1999, activists entered the vessel Maytime at Loch Goil and destroyed equipment by depositing it in the waters of Loch Goil and pouring a mixture of sirup and sand over its machinery.
5 In 2012, activists disarmed thirteen army vehicles by setting them on fire.
6 In 2011, 200 international activists marked the Northern European Aerospace Test Range (NEAT) by entering the base, colouring runways and buildings, and by marking the road leading to it with pink arrows and the slogan 'War starts here, let's stop it here!'. The airspace was marked by a release of pink balloons after a die-in outside the area.
7 In 2003, during then-US President George W. Bush's visit to London, the fountains at Trafalgar Square were dyed with red paint to make them look like pools of blood.
8 In 2011, activists marked the university building with the slogan 'War starts here' to denounce the university's involvement with war and militarisation through its role as a think-tank for military and security studies.
9 In 2012, 800 international activists participated at the NATO Game Over action day near Brussels. 500 activists tried to enter the NATO compound; twenty of them succeeded.
10 In 2012, about 150 activists from the War Starts Here camp entered the GÜZ - the largest German military training ground.
11 The huge variety of strategies to counter the direct recruitment of young people (for example at schools, job centres, universities, and recruitment-offices) are not explored in this article as they are referred to elsewhere in this book.
12 The call-out by the European Antimilitarist Network (EAN), and some activities, are documented at www.wri-irg.org/campaigns/warstartshere. So far the campaign has been quite successful in Germany, where since its beginning in 2011 activists from a broad political spectrum have done a great number of very different actions, from blockading armament production sites and schools visited by recruiting military officials, to

highlighting public military concerts and firms involved in cooperation with the military, and disrupting military equipment. So far, two 'War starts here' action camps have been held - in Sweden (2011) and Germany (2012). Other international 'War starts here' action camps will take place in 2013: in Germany from 21 - 29 July near Letzlingen, and in the UK from 26 August - 7 September at Burghfield.

The need for a queer perspective

Cattis Laska and Hanns Molander

Militarism is not just a war, an army or a fighter jet. Militarism is a system, a logic and a set of norms that perpetuates and recreates our societies and our daily lives. Queer analysis of power is a political tool that can help us to challenge these norms, and thus, to also challenge militarism.

The militarist ideology is deeply rooted in the heterosexist system, which forms social norms for gender/sex and sexuality. Militarism, just as society in general, is based on the construction and assumption of two opposite genders; one in need of protection (feminine) and one that protects (masculine), and their mutual interdependence and attraction. Militarism defines masculinity as powerful and aggressive, and femininity as humble and passive, and thus reproduces the construction of gender/sex. Heterosexism also includes the presumption that most people are heterosexual and that heterosexual relationships are 'normal' and therefore better. These assumptions and prejudices about gender/sex and sexuality have been used, and are used, to marginalise, discriminate and criminalise LGBT (Lesbian, Gay, Bisexual, and Transgender) people who challenge the legitimacy of these norms. To really challenge militarism, we need to challenge gender and sexuality norms, both in society as a whole and within our own movements. And as well as directly challenging the militarist ideology imposed on us, we also need to work on ways to create a truly peaceful and secure world.

This article explores some examples of antimilitarist work that the direct action for peace network Ofog have been doing in Sweden. Counter-recruitment is often the focus of this work.

Workshop for high school classes

Since the military's primary target group for recruitment is 15-25 year olds, high school students are a crucial group for Ofog to work with. We have put together a workshop to discuss war and militarism, mainly directed at high scool classes, but also other groups targeted by military recruitment. Of course, one of the goals of this workshop is to counter recruitment, but it also raises critical awareness about war and militarism in general. From doing these workshops, it has been very clear to us that young people have few ways of getting the information they need in order to make an informed choice on whether to join the military or not, even just in terms what to think of the military and to know what they're really doing. We want to create space for young people to discuss what peace and security mean to them, what they need in order to feel secure, and what their thoughts are on the military.

Actions against the Swedish Armed Forces recruitment campaign 'Have you got what it takes?'

The first recruitment campaign after compulsory military service was abolished used slogans like 'Your grandmother doesn't care if Sweden's air space is violated' and 'Your friend doesn't care if there's a natural disaster', followed by 'Do you have what it takes to have an opinion?'. In this campaign, those presented as not having opinions – as not caring - were never male: they were either female or gender-neutral. And thus 'to have what it takes' was to be male and to challenge these people, as well as to have a macho attitude, to be able to fit into a hierarchy, to have enough physical strength, and to be ready to use violence. Ofog's response to this campaign was to question the truth of the statements, giving the people 'without opinions' another voice that was not passive but active, saying 'We've got what it takes'. But our sense of 'having what it takes' is different – it means nonviolence, non-hierchical structure, equal access to knowledge, and so on.

Stockholm Pride Festival

Military: 'Your grandmother doesn't care if Sweden's air space is violated'
Ofog: 'But on the other hand she's really pissed off that the US Air Force tests bombs in Northern Sweden'

Military: 'What do you think? Do you have what it takes to have an opinion? Test yourself at forsvarsmakten.se'
Ofog: 'We've got what it takes / ofog.org'
(credit - Ofog)

Another example is that the military, both in Sweden and in many other parts of the world, is currently using LGBTQ communities to legitimise their activities. By creating a (false) public image of a 'modern' and 'open' military, they seek to create acceptance for militarism and military 'solutions'. It is very important to organise against this 'pinkwashing' by the military - to refuse to be used to legitimise death and destruction. Together we must show that only an antimilitarist world is a really secure world for LGBTQ people and others.

The Swedish Armed Forces participated in the Stockholm Pride Festival in 2011 with the slogan 'Openness - part of our reality'. This was part of their recruiting campaign 'Welcome to our reality', where they promoted themselves as a challenging, exciting and open workplace. At their tent in the 'Pride Park', Ofog did a die-in with a banner saying 'Your reality kills'. With this we wanted to show what their reality really is: war and death. We also blocked their tent for a few hours, preventing them from recruiting. In the Pride parade, which concludes the Pride festival, the organisation for LGBT soldiers marched in military uniforms by a big truck with the slogan 'Openness - part of our reality'. We walked beside them for the whole parade, holding speech bubbles saying: 'My job kills', 'I'm just as good at killing as heterosexual soldiers' and 'Here I walk defending my human rights, while my job is is about violation of other people's human rights'.

Summer course: 'The militarisation of our lives and societies -

Die-in in Pride Park, Stockholm, 2001. The banner says 'Your reality kills' (credit - Ofog)

feminism as resistance'

Last summer we organised a four-week summer course on the topics of feminism and antimilitarism: how to use feminism as an analytical tool for understanding war and militarism, and how to use feminism as a practical tool or method to stop war. In order to counter militarism and militarisation, we need to understand the connections between patriarchy, gender, war, and militarism. Since much of Ofog's work is focused on direct action, we recognise that we also need space and time for reflection and discussion on what security means to us, and how we can realise it.

It was therefore also important for us to bring 'recruitment by and resistantance by queers' as a theme to the June 2012 Darmstadt conference on the 'Militarisation of youth'. As well as the need for feminist and queer activists need to see the struggle against militarism as a central part of their struggles and movements, antimilitarist activists need to include a queer analysis in their work against war. Besides the many reasons mentioned above, queer youth are especially vulnerable as a target group for military recruitment because of the discrimination and oppression that exclude them or see them kicked out of their schools, homes and workplaces. Those doing counter recruitment work need to be familiar with queer perspectives and issues, and to be sensitive to these.

Because 'queer and antimilitarism' was a new theme to many people who took part in the workshop that we facilitated at Darmstadt, much of the time was spent on explanations, resulting in limited discussion. This demonstrates the need for us to work on this issue, and establish it as a central part of counter recruitment work specifically, as well as of antimilitarism in general.

We need to discuss what we consider to be part of the antimilitarist struggle, how issues considered 'other' (including heterosexism, but also, for example, racism or ableism) can be raised within the antimilitarist movement, and how we can integrate them. We need to respond to the military's appropriation of words and struggles that should be incompatible with it because they are based on human rights (which the military fundamentally contravene). And we need to devise ways of reaching out to members of these groups in risk of being recruited.

The struggles against oppressive structures based on gender/sex and sexuality are essential in the struggle against militarisation. Consequently, we need to continue to work against heterosexism, transphobia and patriarchy, in our own movements and in the rest of the society. And we need a queer perspective, not as something 'extra', but as something that permeates our antimilitarist work.

Notes on the contributors

Sergeiy Sandler: Sergeiy is a conscientious objector to military service, a long-time activist in the Israeli feminist antimilitarist movement New Profile, and a member of the International Council of the War Resisters' International.

David Gee: David has written and co-written various research reports on ethical issues arising from military recruitment: 'Informed Choice? Armed forces recruitment practice in the United Kingdom' (2008), 'Army recruiters visit London's poorest schools most often' (2010), and 'One Step Forward: The case for ending the recruitment of minors by the British armed forces' (2013), and 'Youngest recruits face greatest risks in Afghansitan' (forthcoming). In 2010 he co-founded ForcesWatch. At WRI's Countering the Militarisation of Youth Conference, he was one of those interviewed.

Rafael Uzcátegui: Rafael is part of an anarchist collective that since 1995 has produced the newspaper El Libertario (The Libertarian), which has a circulation of around 2000. Campaigning against militarism has always been a very important theme for the paper, but unfortunately this has been the only antimilitarist initiative in Venezuela in the past thirteen years. He is interested in the targetted militarisation of children and young people because he thinks that what they are exposed to in these formative years will determine their values and beliefs in their adult lives. His article in this book is based loosely on a piece he wrote for the WRI's Countering the Militarisation of Youth Conference Reader. At the conference he gave a talk on the same topic, and he was also one of those interviewed.

Michael Schulze von Glaßer: Michael has been concerned with military advertising in the public sphere since 2008. He has published two books on the German Armed Forces' engagement with children. He is on the board of Informationsstelle Militarisierung (Information Centre on Militarisation), for whom he has done several studies on the portrayal of military operations in video games and on the connection between the games industry, arms industry and the military. At WRI's Countering the Militarisation of Youth Conference he was on a panel exploring different perspectives on militarisation, approaching it from a public spaces and military culture angle, and led a workshop discussion on military video games. He also conducted all of the video interviews, extracts of the transcripts of which are included in this book. His article on public space was based on a piece he wrote for the conference Reader.

Ruti Kantor and Diana Dolev: Ruti has been a member of New Profile since 2000. She is a Visual Communication Designer and a lecturer at the Bezalel Academy of Art and Design in Jerusalem. Her Design and political activist background have informed her interest in militaristic images in the every day life in Israel. Diana has been a member of New Profile for about thirteen years, which has been an ongoing learning process of the appearances and effects of militarism on civil society. As an architectural historian, she has a special interest in the design of urban spaces and its interelations with militaristic trends in urban environments. At WRI's Countering the Militarisation of Youth Conference Ruti and Diana facilitated a workshop on military and public spaces, which inspired their article in this book.

Boro Kitanoski: Boro is a peace activist from the Republic of Macedonia. He was a conscientious objector to military service. He now focuses on 'Dealing with the past' work - collecting life stories, and engaging military veterans, victims, and other actors in peace processes - in Macedonia and former Yugoslavia. At WRI's Countering the Militarisation of Youth Conference he gave a presentation on the militarisation of youth in former Yugoslavia.

Jorge Vélez: Jorge is a member of the Medellín Antimilitarist and Feminist Network, where he leads a training Anti-patriarchal Training course for young men and women. He is also part of the campaign against police brutality. At WRI's Countering the Militarisation of Youth Conference he gave a presentation on the social and armed conflict in Colombia, outlining the armed groups involved, and their social, political and economic interests, as well as the continuation of forced recruitment and the targeting of poor neighbourhoods by military recruiters, and the status of conscientious objection. He was also interviewed there. His article is an an edited extract of his essay 'Militarización en Colombia: Rasgos históricos, efectos de la guerra y para-estado / Patriarcado, capitalismo y militarismo'.

Jonna Schürkes: Jonna works for Informationsstelle Militarisierung in Germany. Since 1996 they have critically approached the increasing militarisation in Germany and within the European Union. She regards herself as a mediator between the peace movement and critical research on peace and conflict. For a number of years she has been examining the relationship of cuts in social services and recruitment, advertising, and the deployment of youth officers in schools by the German Armed Forces. She has published numerous articles on these topics. At WRI's Countering the Militarisation of Youth Conference she gave a talk on Informationsstelle Militarisierung and its work.

Serdar M. Değirmencioğlu: Serdar is a professor of psychology, a public scholar, and an outspoken advocate of children's rights in Turkey. His work involves activism and focuses on neglected or untouchable issues, such as militarisation of young people. He regards militarism as a serious threat to children's rights, social justice, and peace. The militarism in schools parts of his article are based on a piece he wrote for The Broken Rifle 88 (2011). He has edited a book examing martyrdom and militarism in Turkey, which is to be published in autumn 2013.

Dan Contreras: Dan is part of the Chilean antimilitarist group Ni Casco Ni Uniforme (Neither Helmet Nor Uniform). As an anarchist, researcher and history teacher, he is interested in the in-depth study of military practices in society, specifically in institutions that don't appear to be sources of militarism, such as the education system. His research also encompasses militarism in Latin America and studying the construction of social concepts tied to military culture. At WRI's Countering the Militarisation of Youth Conference he gave a talk which described and analysed some examples of military training in Chilean society and the influence of militarisation on young people today, taking into account its historical origins, its effects and potential responses. He was also one of those interviewed at the conference.

Emma Sangster: Emma is coordinator of ForcesWatch, which questions the ethics of UK military recruitment and the climate of uncritical national pride in the armed forces. At WRI's

Countering the Militarisation of Youth Conference, she sat on the panel exploring different perspectives on militarisation, where she talked about education and recruitment, and co-led a workshop with Ralf Willinger on the Military in Education, which explored how to counter the military's engagement with schoolchildren. Her article in this book is based loosely on a piece she wrote for The Broken Rifle 92 (2012).

Andreas Speck: Andreas worked for WRI's Right to Refuse to Kill programme for more than eleven years. He initiated WRI's Countering the Militarisation of Youth project. His article is based on a talk he gave at WRI's Countering the Militarisation of Youth Conference, where he also provided a queer/gender perspective on a panel discussing how to analyse militarisation, and facilitated a workshop with a similar focus. An article he wrote for The Broken Rifle 85 (2010) was included in the conference Reader.

Sahar Vardi: Sahar Vardi is an Israeli anti-militarism activist, currently working for the American Friends Service Committee coordinating their Israel programme. At eighteen, she refused her mandatory military service. Since then she has been working with movements such as New Profile and the Shministim, to support other young people who resist conscription. She co-wrote a piece for the WRI's Countering the Militarisation of Youth Conference Reader. At the conference she gave a presentation on the use of women to promote conscription in Israel, upon which her article is based. She was also one of those interviewed there.

Kai-Uwe Dosch, Sarah Roßa and Lena Sachs: Kai-Uwe has been working both as a volunteer in the peace movement and as a professional in educational settings for a long time. His stated aim and hope is to counter the intensified militarisation of schools. This has become his 'natural' focus in his present job for the Federation for Social Defense. Sarah became involved in the working group for a Zivilklausel at the University of Frankfurt in 2011. A Zivilklausel is the self-imposed obligation of the university not to cooperate in any way with the armed forces or enterprises producing weapons. In January 2013 the Zivilklausel was undertaken fully by the university. Lena has a BA in Education and an MA in Education and Social Work. She is author of 'Die Zusammenarbeit zwischen Bundeswehr und Schulen - eine kritische Analyse' ('Collaboration between the German Armed Forces and schools - a critical analysis', published in 2012), and coordinates the Baden-Württemberg campaign 'Armed Forces-free Schools'. At WRI's Countering the Militarisation of Youth Conference, Kai-Uwe, Sarah, and Lena co-facilitated a workshop on resistance to militarisation in educational institutions, the discussions and conclusions of which their article in this book is based upon.

Kelly Dougherty: Kelly served in the U.S. military for eight years. She joined the Colorado Army National Guard as a medic in 1996, age 17. She later received training as a Military Police person and was deployed in this role on a peacekeeping mission in Hungary and Croatia from 1999-2000. In 2003 she was deployed with the Military Police to Kuwait and Iraq for year. After returning from Iraq in 2004, she met several other Iraq veterans who were opposed to the U.S. occupation there at a Veterans For Peace convention. She co-founded Iraq Veterans Against the War with them later that year. IVAW currently has about 1,200 members and is actively working on the Operation Recovery and Right to Heal campaigns. At

WRI's Countering the Militarisation of Youth Conference Kelly ran a workshop on the role veterans can play in challenging the militarisation of youth. She was also one of those interviewed there.

Ralf Willinger: Ralf has had a long career working for human rights, peace, refugee advocacy and child welfare in many parts of the world, including Southern Africa and countries in Southeast Asia and Latin America. In addition to his full-time job as Child Rights Officer at Terre des Hommes, Germany, he is the coordinator of the German Coalition to Stop the Use of Child Soldiers. At WRI's Countering the Militarisation of Youth Conference he co-led a workshop with Emma Sangster on the Military in Education, which explored how to counter the military's engagement with schoolchildren. He also co-led a workshop with Helen Kearney on Child Rights.

Cecil Arndt: Cecil is an activist living in Germany, engaged in various antimilitarist groups and networks. He works with dfg-vk (the German section of WRI), and with the European Antimilitarist Network, which currently includes different groups and organisations from six European countries working together in different kinds of campaigns and direct action, and inviting other groups to join them. At WRI's Countering the Militarisation of Youth Conference, he ran a workshop on direct action as resistance to the militarisation of youth, the discussions of which helped inform his article in this book.

Cattis Laska and Hanns Molander: Cattis is a social worker - working mainly with young people - and an activist involved in antimilitarist, asylum rights/No Borders, feminist, queer and prison struggles. Hanns is a disability worker, and is involved in anarchist activism and in the People's Kitchen movement. Both are active in the Swedish antimilitarist network Ofog, which has mainly worked with nonviolent direct actions against the military-industrial complex (arms factories, military exercises, NATO), but since the end of compulsory military service in Sweden in 2010 and the Armed Forces' shift to aggressive recruitment has identified counter recruitment as a very important area of antimilitarist work. Their article in this book is based on a piece they wrote for The Broken Rifle 92 (2012), and on the presentation and workshop they gave at WRI's Countering the Militarisation of Youth Conference. Cattis was also one of those interviewed at the conference.

Resources

WRI's website on youth militarisation and resisting it -
http://antimili-youth.net/

WRI's Countering the Militarisation of Youth project -
http://wri-irg.org/programmes/militarisationofyouth

Countering the Militarisation of Youth 2012 conference Reader -
http://wri-irg.org/militarisationofyouth/DarmstadtReader

The Broken Rifle 92 ('Countering the Militarisation of Youth', 2012) -
http://wri-irg.org/pubs/br92-en.htm

The Broken Rifle 88 ('Military Out of Schools', 2011) -
http://wri-irg.org/pubs/br88-en.htm

WRI's Militarisation of Youth survey data and analysis –
http://wri-irg.org/surveydata

Online discussions on how to combat the militarisation of young people -
www.newtactics.org/conversation/tactics-combating-militarisation

The National Network Opposing the Militarisation of Youth (NNOMY) -
www.facebook.com/NNOMYfriends

Stop Recruiting Kids campaign -
www.facebook.com/StopRecruitingKids

New Profile -
http://newprofile.org/english

ForcesWatch -
http://forceswatch.net

Lernen Für den Frieden -
www.lernenfuerdenfrieden.de/

Desmilitaritzem l'Educació -
http://desmilitaritzem.blog.pangea.org/

Other War Resisters' International publications

Handbook for Nonviolent Campaigns

ISBN 978-0-903517-21-8
January 2009, 152 pages, £5

Social change doesn't just happen. It's the result of the work of committed people striving for a world of justice and peace. This work gestates in groups or cells of activists, in discussions, in training sessions, in reflecting on previous experiences, in planning, in experimenting, and in learning from others. Preparing ourselves for our work for social justice is key to its success.

This Handbook shares what people have already developed in different contexts.

Women Conscientious Objectors - An Anthology

Edited by Ellen Elster and Majken Jul Sørensen
ISBN 978-0-903517-22-5
2010, 154 pages, £8

This anthology reflects WRI's continued commitment to bring together and support women conscientious objectors and to address issues of gender and militarism, both in WRI's staffed programmes — the Right to Refuse to Kill, and Nonviolence for Change (promoting nonviolent action to remove the causes of war) — and more generally throughout the WRI network.

Go to http://wri-irg.org for more information

About War Resisters' International

War Resisters' International was founded in 1921 under the name "Paco". It was and is based on the WRI declaration:

> War is a crime against humanity. I am therefore determined not to support any kind of war, and to strive for the removal of all causes of war.

War Resisters' International exists to promote nonviolent action against the causes of war, and to support and connect people around the world who refuse to take part in war or the preparation of war. On this basis, WRI works for a world without war.

Nonviolence

WRI embraces nonviolence. For some, nonviolence is a way of life. For all of us, it is a form of action that affirms life, speaks out against oppression, and acknowledges the value of each person.

Nonviolence can combine active resistance, including civil disobedience, with dialogue; it can combine noncooperation — withdrawal of support from a system of oppression — with constructive work to build alternatives.

As a way of engaging in conflict, nonviolence attempts to empower those at the bottom of society and include people from different sides in seeking a solution.

No to war

WRI will never endorse any kind of war, whether it is waged by a state, by a 'liberation army', or under the auspices of the United Nations, or even if it is called a 'humanitarian military intervention'. Wars, however noble the rhetoric, invariably are used to serve some power-political or economic interest. We know where war leads — to suffering and destruction, to rape and organised crime, to betrayal of values and to new structures of domination.

Contact:

War Resisters' International
5 Caledonian Road
London N1 9DX
Britain
Email info@wri-irg.org
Web http://wri-irg.org